Advanced Image–Based Spam Detection and Filtering Techniques

Sunita Vikrant Dhavale
Defense Institute of Advanced Technology (DIAT), Pune, India

A volume in the Advances in
Information Security, Privacy, and
Ethics (AISPE) Book Series

www.igi-global.com

Published in the United States of America by
 IGI Global
 Information Science Reference (an imprint of IGI Global)
 701 E. Chocolate Avenue
 Hershey PA, USA 17033
 Tel: 717-533-8845
 Fax: 717-533-8661
 E-mail: cust@igi-global.com
 Web site: http://www.igi-global.com

Library of Congress Cataloging-in-Publication Data

Names: Dhavale, Sunita Vikrant, author.
Title: Advanced image-based spam detection and filtering techniques / by
 Sunita Vikrant Dhavale.
Description: Hershey, PA : Information Science Reference, [2017] | Includes
 bibliographical references and index.
Identifiers: LCCN 2016058440| ISBN 9781683180135 (hardcover) | ISBN
 9781683180142 (ebook)
Subjects: LCSH: Spam filtering (Electronic mail) | Digital images--Security
 measures.
Classification: LCC TK5105.743 D46 2017 | DDC 005.8/2--dc23 LC record available at https://
lccn.loc.gov/2016058440

This book is published in the IGI Global book series Advances in Information Security, Privacy, and Ethics (AISPE) (ISSN: 1948-9730; eISSN: 1948-9749)

British Cataloguing in Publication Data
A Cataloguing in Publication record for this book is available from the British Library.

All work contributed to this book is new, previously-unpublished material.
The views expressed in this book are those of the authors, but not necessarily of the publisher.

For electronic access to this publication, please contact: eresources@igi-global.com.

Advances in Information Security, Privacy, and Ethics (AISPE) Book Series

ISSN:1948-9730
EISSN:1948-9749

Editor-in-Chief: Manish Gupta, State University of New York, USA

MISSION

As digital technologies become more pervasive in everyday life and the Internet is utilized in ever increasing ways by both private and public entities, concern over digital threats becomes more prevalent.

The **Advances in Information Security, Privacy, & Ethics (AISPE) Book Series** provides cutting-edge research on the protection and misuse of information and technology across various industries and settings. Comprised of scholarly research on topics such as identity management, cryptography, system security, authentication, and data protection, this book series is ideal for reference by IT professionals, academicians, and upper-level students.

COVERAGE

- Access Control
- Information Security Standards
- IT Risk
- Tracking Cookies
- Risk Management
- Technoethics
- Electronic Mail Security
- Network Security Services
- Security Classifications
- Privacy-Enhancing Technologies

IGI Global is currently accepting manuscripts for publication within this series. To submit a proposal for a volume in this series, please contact our Acquisition Editors at Acquisitions@igi-global.com or visit: http://www.igi-global.com/publish/.

Titles in this Series

For a list of additional titles in this series, please visit:
http://www.igi-global.com/book-series/advances-information-security-privacy-ethics/37157

Securing Government Information and Data in Developing Countries
Saleem Zoughbi (UN APCICT, UN ESCAP, South Korea)
Information Science Reference ● ©2017 ● 307pp ● H/C (ISBN: 9781522517030) ● US $160.00

Security Breaches and Threat Prevention in the Internet of Things
N. Jeyanthi (VIT University, India) and R. Thandeeswaran (VIT University, India)
Information Science Reference ● ©2017 ● 276pp ● H/C (ISBN: 9781522522966) ● US $180.00

Decentralized Computing Using Blockchain Technologies and Smart Contracts...
S. Asharaf (Indian Institute of Information Technology and Management, Kerala, India)
and S. Adarsh (Indian Institute of Information Technology and Management, Kerala, India)
Information Science Reference ● ©2017 ● 128pp ● H/C (ISBN: 9781522521938) ● US $120.00

Cybersecurity Breaches and Issues Surrounding Online Threat Protection
Michelle Moore (George Mason University, USA)
Information Science Reference ● ©2017 ● 408pp ● H/C (ISBN: 9781522519416) ● US $195.00

Security Solutions and Applied Cryptography in Smart Grid Communications
Mohamed Amine Ferrag (Guelma University, Algeria) and Ahmed Ahmim (University of
Larbi Tebessi, Algeria)
Information Science Reference ● ©2017 ● 464pp ● H/C (ISBN: 9781522518297) ● US $215.00

Threat Mitigation and Detection of Cyber Warfare and Terrorism Activities
Maximiliano E. Korstanje (University of Palermo, Argentina)
Information Science Reference ● ©2017 ● 315pp ● H/C (ISBN: 9781522519386) ● US $190.00

Online Banking Security Measures and Data Protection
Shadi A. Aljawarneh (Jordan University of Science and Technology, Jordan)
Information Science Reference ● ©2017 ● 312pp ● H/C (ISBN: 9781522508649) ● US $215.00

For an enitre list of titles in this series, please visit:
http://www.igi-global.com/book-series/advances-information-security-privacy-ethics/37157

www.igi-global.com

701 East Chocolate Avenue, Hershey, PA 17033, USA
Tel: 717-533-8845 x100 ● Fax: 717-533-8661
E-Mail: cust@igi-global.com ● www.igi-global.com

Table of Contents

Preface

Welcome to the interesting world of image-based spam detection techniques! In last few years, we have all experienced the huge spam images stepping easily inside our mailboxes; thus increasing our frustration level towards existing email services. Spam technology, which was invented long back in order to send one mail to everyone; nowadays, has brought huge frustrations for all email users. The reader should remember that each technology comes with some associated hidden and challenging problems; for which we need to prepare ourselves. Although, the right to send the email to any known or unknown email address has been exploited effectively by the spammers, we, the genuine internet users, do have the right to decide which mails can enter in our mailboxes. And this book can be viewed as our sincere step towards protecting our inbox from such unwanted emails.

While most of the existing email spam detectors deal with text based spam, image-based spam raises a new set of questions, techniques and solutions. Due to its high-volume nature and more network resource consumption property, image-based spam is becoming a new threat to the Internet and its users. Hence, recently many researchers are focussing this problem domain. In future, new applications will be built on top of existing detection systems in order to deal with all kinds of spam messages effectively.

This book serves as a professional reference to provide today's most complete and concise view of image-based spam detection techniques available. It offers in-depth coverage of image spam, available filtering techniques, and practices as they relate to established technologies as well as recent advancements. It explores novel image features and image spam detection solutions. Individual chapters address the existing challenges with each available technique. The primary audience for this book consists of researchers and practitioners in industry and academia as well as security technologists and engineers working with or interested in spam detection. This comprehensive reference will also be of value to undergraduate and graduate-level engineering students. The reader requires a basic understanding of communication and rough knowledge of internet or networking in general. This book tries to cover many aspects of image-based spam detection from a computer science point of view. If reader is interested in more detailed information regarding certain topic, he or she will find many pointers to research publications or related websites.

Of course, the technical discussions and information given in this book can be used for both good and bad, and some might use this book as a manual for generating more resistant image based spams for attacking our email inboxes. That's both true and unfortunate, but the trade-off is worth it. It's the genuine email users who need to know how image spams are generated, what are the future consequences posed by them, and what are the limitations and vulnerabilities exhibited by existing image based spam detection techniques. The more people who know about these limitations, there will be a better chance for carrying out the research to fix these problems.

This book is designed to take the reader through a logical progression for a foundational understanding of today's spam world. The book is composed of total seven chapters, as well as three appendices, including discussion on existing tools available and compilation of code snippets. Chapter 1 sets the stage for the rest of the book by presenting insight into the secrets and tricks that are used by spammers to evade from anti-spam techniques. The chapter also states various techniques to handle spam along with the corresponding existing laws and regulations. Finally, this chapter has exposed the dark side of image spam. Chapter 2 provides an overview of image-based spam. This chapter establishes rules to carry out a preliminary analysis to describe a spam mail. The chapter also brings out the limitations of existing spam detection techniques to handle image-based spam. Finally it provides the details of the image spam dataset which are publicly available for the researchers and the detailed analysis of these spam databases. Chapter 3 describes various features related to color, shape, texture, metadata domain of image-based spam in detail. The chapter discussion also focus that image spam detection can be seen as a multi disciplinary area comprising of image analysis, machine learning techniques, and artificial intelligent techniques.

Chapter 4 provides the detailed overview of OCR method and a thorough literature review on spam filters based on OCR methods. The chapter brings out the limitations of existing spam detection techniques based on OCR methods to handle image-based spam. Finally, it provides the detailed comparison of these techniques. Chapter 5 provides the detailed overview of spam detection methods based on near duplicate detection schemes. The chapter also brings out the limitations of these spam detection techniques. Finally, it provides the detailed comparison of these techniques. Chapter 6 provides the detailed overview of spam detection methods based on different visual features. The chapter also brings out the detailed literature review of existing visual feature based spam detection techniques. The chapter proposes new feature related to metadata, noise and texture domain which can be exploited for spam detection. Further, the chapter proposes a novel server-client image spam detection model based on novel texture feature using GW-LPQ. The strength of image features for image spam detection is proved with the experimental results.

Chapter 7 proposes a server side solution F-ISDS that demonstrates the application of Fuzzy Inference System for effective image spam detection. Experimental results confirm the efficacy of the proposed solution with zero False Positive Rate. The accuracy of detection may be enhanced in future either by integrating IP tracing techniques and/or investigating more discriminative spam image features. Finally, the book provides supplemental materials including the snippets of code used during experimentation in Appendix A, followed by an elaborated discussions on existing tools and techniques from the text in Appendix B.

You are encouraged to send any comments regarding the book to sunitadhavale75@rediffmail.com. Finally, I hope you enjoy reading this book and forgive me for simplifications I have used to avoid blurring the big picture of spam detection field. Many such details may change as research evolves over time and truly speaking, research work in any domain is never said to be finished completely.

Sunita Vikrant Dhavale
Defense Institute of Advanced Technology (DIAT), Pune, India

Acknowledgment

This book would not have occurred if not for the support and encouragement of many entities. I hope I have covered them all here and apologize for any omissions by mistake.

First and foremost, I would like to thank Lord Ganesha, for giving me the strength, knowledge, ability and opportunity to undertake this research book writing., I thank to my loving husband Vikrant, my son Amit, my daugther Aditi, my father Govindrao and my mother Leela for being so supportive throughout this book project. Their understanding and support was crucial to us completing this book.

Secondly, I thank to my organization Defence Insitute of Technology, Girinagar, Pune, *Dr. Surendra Pal, Honourable Vice Chancellor, DIAT, Pune* and *Dr. S. E. Talole, Dean (Technology), DIAT, Pune* for providing good research facilities for carrying out the required experiments for the related research areas. I also thank to Dr. Rajendra Deodhar, Mr. Udit Jain, Mr. Mohit Verma and all anonymous reviewers whose valuable suggestions and comments helped me to enhance the quality of my book. Finally, I thank to all who inspired me throughout my life in all positive ways.

Big thanks must also go to the tireless International Publisher of Progressive Information Science and Technology Research, IGI Global publisher, editors and production team who worked on the book, including Jan Travers, Kelsey Weitzel-Leishman and Maria Rohde. And finally, a tremendous "Thank You" to all of the intended readers, whose support will help me in future book writings.

Sunita Vikrant Dhavale
Defense Institute of Advanced Technology (DIAT), Pune, India

Chapter 1
Image Spam:
A Call to Action

ABSTRACT

In order to understand the never-ending fights between developers of anti-spam detection techniques and the spammers; it is important to have an insight of the history of spam mails. On May 3, 1978, Gary Thuerk, a marketing manager at Digital Equipment Corporation sent his first mass email to more than 400 customers over the Arpanet in order to promote and sell Digital's new T-Series of VAX systems (Streitfeld, 2003). In this regard, he said, "It's too much work to send everyone an e-mail. So we'll send one e-mail to everyone". He said with pride, "I was the pioneer. I saw a new way of doing things." As every coin has two sides, any technology too can be utilized for good and bad intention. At that time, Gary Thuerk would have never dreamt of this method of sending mails to emerge as an area of research in future. Gary Thuerk ended up getting crowned as the father of spam mails instead of the father of e-marketing. In the present scenario, the internet receives 2.5 billion pieces of spam a day by spiritual followers of Thuerk.

DOI: 10.4018/978-1-68318-013-5.ch001

1.1. INTRODUCTION

Spam mail is also known as junk mail, unsolicited commercial email (UCE) or unsolicited bulk Email (UBE). It is named after Spam - a brand of canned precooked meat products, which is portrayed as tasting nasty, ubiquitous -as included in every dish and unavoidable in the Monty Python comedy sketch in 1970. Hence, the word Spam came to be transferred by analogy.

Technically, spam mail is defined as "Unsolicited, unwanted email that was sent indiscriminately, directly or indirectly, by a sender having no current relationship with the recipient" (Sanz, HidalgoGomez, & PerezCortizo, 2008). It exhibits following important properties:

- **Unsolicited:** The information in the mail is not at all important for the addressee.
- **Unknown Sender:** The sender is not known to the recipient.
- **Massive:** These are sent in batches to many receivers at the same time.

Spam would not be so bad, if it was not quite so voluminous, offensive and annoying (Dynamic web Solutions, 2016). Unfortunately, today it has become a prevalent problem in the Internet world. Unsolicited email marketing exploits spam e-mail for commercial purposes to deliver information about various products. Spam includes bogus offers that could cost us time and money. One such example is Jeremy Jaynes, one of the spammers who earned $24 million by selling fake goods, services, and pornography via spam. He was arrested in December 2003 and convicted in November 2004.

Typically spam offers some doubtful job offers, financial service, impotence treatments and invitations to pornographic web sites (Dynamic web Solutions, 2016). Figure 1 shows some of the sample spam mails from personal account which are collected during month of June 2016. Day by day, they are getting successful in convincing the people to respond to these fake offers. Recent survey shows that both educated and uneducated people are easily getting trapped in the fake offers contained in spam messages. Spam e-mail may also include malwares or other executable file attachments. In reality, most people can live without this constant barrage of offensive unsolicited e-mail (Dynamic web Solutions, 2016). Moreover, a quality and productive time

Figure 1. Sample spam mails

of employees is wasted in reading and deleting these spam from their mail inbox, thus affecting organization's time, productivity and bandwidth severely.

According to the Message Anti-Abuse Working Group, the amount of spam e-mails in the first half of 2014 was approximately 90% (Maawg, 2011) of the total e-mails. Figure 2 shows the spam volume over a period of one year from March 2014 to March 2015 as reported by Symantec (Symantec, 2014).

Figure 2. Spam messages vs Total messages (Symantec, 2014)

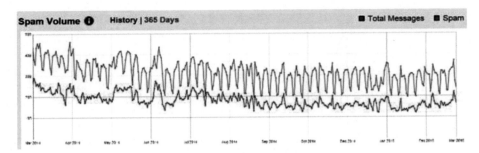

1.2. HOW SPAMMER WORKS?

Spam is produced and shaped by spammers; who belong to many different populations around the world such as, programmers, attackers, criminals, terrorists, bots, merchants, marketers, corrupt bankers, cops, lawyers, security professionals, and hackers. In reality, no one ever admits to being a spammer. Today's spammers change the source continuously and send spam from multiple infected machines or servers. Shutting down or blocking few infected servers doesn't affect the flow of spam to any great effect. Spammers work like revolutionary war soldiers making everybody think they're fighting an army of 5000, when it's really only five guys.

In a typical scenario, an advertising agency or promoter enters into an agreement with the spammer and the spammer in turn sends email advertisements to a group of unwary recipients. As sending the spam is economical than sending postal bulk mailings, this practice is followed by most of the promoters.

In order to send spam, spammers need to obtain the email addresses of the intended recipients. They use email harvester tools that mine e-mail addresses from newsgroups and web sites (Dynamic web Solutions, 2016). The email harvesters collect names from websites, newsgroups, mailing lists, or other services in which users identify themselves by email address. These tools generally search for special symbols or keywords like "@" symbol, ".com", ".org" etc. Generally, these email addresses are collected by spammers without the consent of the address owners. Some spammers obtain email addresses from third party without the consent of the address owners. Some spammers guess email addresses and send a test message or a real spam to guessed addresses. They analyze the response to sent mail. Reception of an error message or confirmation in return by email indicates the validity of guessed email address. The validity of email addresses collected during email harvesting process is also confirmed using the same technique. Sometimes sending back the spam to the sender by mail client software also confirms the validity of email addresses. In some systems, if the recipient clicks on an unsubscribe link, that may cause that email address to be marked as valid (Absolute Astronomy, 2016). In this case, a recipient automatically assumes that clicking on the unsubscribe link is provided only to unsubscribe to the messages they no longer wish to receive.

1.3. SPAMMER TRICKS

Almost all ISPs, internet users and system administrators deploy different techniques to block, filter, or expel spam from users' mailboxes (Absolute Astronomy, 2016). In order to overcome these measures, spammers utilize different techniques to deliver the spam emails.

1. **Webmail:** Spammers create accounts on free webmail services, such as Gmail or Hotmail, to send spam or to receive e-mailed responses from potential customers. They use several e-mail accounts to send mass mails and web bots to automate the creation of these accounts.

2. **Internet Hoaxes:** These messages are circulated by email that encourages the users to pass them to other users. They may contain warning messages about latest non-existent viruses, messages asking monitory help for a person dying of cancer, or email messages containing words like 'forward this email to everyone you know …', 'send 10 dollars to this account…and become millionaire in six weeks…' etc. These messages are fabricated so well that user can tempted to circulate them and end up in generating more network traffic and hence, more economic losses.

3. **Third-Party Computers:** As soon as a spam source is identified by IP address filtering methods (Goodman, 2007), Internet Service Providers (ISPs) can blacklist the related IP addresses. ISPs block spammer's accounts after receiving the complaints from the recipients. To avoid such a situation, spammers utilize someone else's computer or network connection to send spam. Hence, tracking the spammers becomes complex task for investigators or law enforcement agencies. The exponential rise in number of unprotected computers that are online makes the situation even worse. The group of such compromised computers is known as botnet and is utilized by the spammers to churn out millions of messages

per day (Absolute Astronomy, 2016). Some of the examples of third party computers utilized by spammers are as follows:

a. **Open Relays:** An open mail relay is an SMTP (Simple Mail Transfer Protocol) server configured which allows any user on the Internet to send e-mail to any known or unknown user. This was the default configuration used in many mail servers initially. Spammers can select such mail server/open relay (say, mail.abc.org with SMTP listening port 25) that offers unrestricted relay of SMTP messages to send spam mail using a file (sample spam_message.txt given here) containing desired SMTP commands and message along with the netcat tool (command –nc invokes this tool) to pipe the output of file to such relays. where, spam_message.txt may contain following SMTP commands and message, Later, open mail relays became unpopular because of their exploitation by spammers and worms. Many relays were blacklisted by other servers. By 2003, less than 1% of corporate mail servers were available as open relays, down from 91% in 1997 (Absolute Astronomy, 2016).

b. **Open Proxies:** After the blacklisting of open relays by many organizations, spammers resorted to other tactics, most prominently the use of open proxies (Absolute Astronomy, 2016). A proxy offers a computer network service to allow clients to make indirect network connections to other network services as shown in Figure 3. In case of open proxy, once a client requests to the open proxy for network services, it will create connections for any client to any server, without authentication. This feature of open proxies offered greater flexibility to the spammers, as the spammers could exploit this feature to direct such open proxies to connect to any mail server to send the spam through them. Also, as the mail server would log a connection from the proxy and not with the spammer computer, this provided an even greater degree of concealment for the spammer than an open relay (Absolute Astronomy, 2016).

c. **Web Scripts:** Besides relays and proxies, spammers can use other insecure services to send spam. One example is FormMail.pl, a common gateway interface (CGI) script to allow Web-site users to send e-mail feedback from an HTML form. Such scripts allow users to redirect e-mail to arbitrary addresses. Spam sent through open FormMail scripts is frequently marked by the program's characteristic opening line: "Below is the result of your feedback form." Some websites offer the feature called 'tell a friend about

Figure 3. Open Proxy

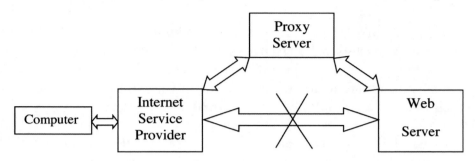

this page' which may be vulnerable by design and may allow the visitor to add their message to the email that is sent. Consequently, such scripts are often abused to send spam.

d. **Spammer Viruses:** In 2003, spammers began creating their own tools/viruses which were capable of deploying proxies and other spam-sending tools. The widespread change from Windows 9x to Windows XP for many home computers in 2003, greatly accelerated the use of home computers to act as remotely controlled spam proxies. The original version of Windows XP had several major vulnerabilities that allowed the machines to be compromised over a network connection without requiring actions on the part of the user or owner (Absolute Astronomy, 2016). Instead of sending spam from one source, today's spammers send spam from multiple zombies (zombie is a private computer on internet which is infected with malicious software and controlled without the owners' knowledge by attackers) in a botnet (botnet is a network of zombies). Losing one zombie doesn't affect the flow of spam to any great effect.

4. **Obfuscation Methods:** Spammers also try different message obfuscation methods in order to escape from spam filters. The message contents are obscured using different techniques like splitting messages by using delimiters or any other characters (say; the word VIAGRA can be written as V-I:A,G*R;A), HTML tags or comments (like; VI</n>AGRA), different encodings (for example; V1AGR4), adding randomly normal good words in the spam content in order to make it difficult for spam filters to extract main features of the content. The efficiency of spam filter gets affected using these techniques.

1.4. SPAM IS ONLY GETTING WORSE

According to the Message Anti-Abuse Working Group (MAAWG), the amount of spam mails in the first half of 2014 was approximately 90% of total e-mails. Survey carried out in 2009 reveals that in order to prevent the spam the total expenditure incurred was 130 billion U.S. dollars. The depressing effects of spam are as follows (Rahul, 2016),

1. **Loss of Efficiency:** Spam consumes a considerable proportion of all e-mail traffic, huge amounts of network bandwidth, memory, storage space etc. It also forces internet users and system administrators to spend their productive time for reading, deleting, filtering, and blocking spam etc. These resources otherwise could have been used for the legitimate work.

2. **Financial Loss:** In 2009, a survey revealed that in order to prevent the spam, the total expenditure incurred was 130 billion U.S. dollars. Spammers use spam mails to cheat people out of their confidential information, to deliver spiteful software, or to cause a temporary failure of a mail server. This can indirectly incur financial loss to either end users or organizations. Spammers may engage in deliberate fraud by using fake names, addresses, and other contact information.

3. **Breaching Into Somebody Life:** Spammers by sending spam, encroaches somebody's private life. It irritates, annoy and divert the attention of the individual by distracting him from his important job. It forces users to watch unwanted materials like pornography. Spam messages can affect social harmony. Criminals use spam message to spread rumors and to provoke ethnic hatred, which influences the social communism.

4. **Objectionable Contents:** Most of the spam contains objectionable contents like commercial messages promoting doubtful schemes, messages containing sexually explicit material, messages containing harmful embedded code or hostile file attachments etc.

5. **Threat to Internet Security:** Spam can contain harmful malicious software, virus, trojan etc. which can exploit computers and network systems. Spam has become primary means of performing phishing and

fraud attacks by stealing valid credentials from bank users. In phishing attacks, high volumes of spam are sent to millions of e-mail accounts with the expectation that only a small percentage need to succeed. A success rate as low as 1% still means on average 10,000 passwords for every million messages.

6. **Damage to Reputation:** Generally, spammers compromise mail servers to send copies of a message to a long list of recipients. This unauthorized third-party relaying damages the reputation of company whose mail server is compromised by spammers.

1.5. APPROACHES TO HANDLE SPAM

Based on actions carried out by individual users or website administrators, various anti-spam techniques are suggested in literature to prevent email spam.

1.5.1. Restriction on Availability of Email Addresses

Individual users can emphasis on restricting the availability of their email addresses to spammers using simple methods like sharing an email address only among a limited group of concerned people, listing the recipient names after "bcc:" instead of after "to:" while forwarding the emails and avoiding to send any response to the spam.

In order to protect the posted email addresses from email harvesters, users can replace special symbols like "@" symbol with string "_at_" or "." symbol with string "_dot_", so that only human can interpret them. The email addresses can also be represented in picture or image format instead of pure text form which makes it difficult to read by email harvesters (Dynamic Web Solutions, 2016). Both of these techniques are easy to setup. We can also use javascript to encode the email address to be displayed on webpage in order protect it from email harvesters. A simple harvester foiling javascript as given below can be inserted into the html code, where we want the email link to be appeared.

```
<html>
................
<script language="JavaScript" type="text/JavaScript">
var first = "chairman"
var  second = "@"
var third = "abccompany.com"
document.write('<a href=\"mailto:' + first + second +
third +'\">Click here to send email to us</a>');
</script>
..............
</html>
```

This script encodes the actual email address into different parts (say, "chairman" and "abccompany.com"). When user opens the page, the script runs to join these parts together, which will display the link that looks like 'click here to send email to us' when the user opens the page. This makes our email address is still visible in the source code, but it's unlikely that any harvester will recognize it. For displaying multiple email address, we can define a function in an external javascript file. This technique is relatively simple but it needs javascript to be enabled at client side.

Websites can also use poisoner (a software that "poisons" the harvester), filters, and blocking software. These softwares generate fake email addresses or direct the harvester to a nonexistent site. Nowadays, many websites provide contact forms that allow users to send email indirectly by filling out forms in a web browser to avoid spam. These techniques are robust and safe but difficult to setup.

1.5.2. Anti-Spam Detection Techniques (Metsis, Androutsopoulos, & Paliouras, 2006)

The Internet Engineering Task Force (IETF) adopted Simple Mail Transfer Protocol (SMTP) as de facto standards for internet email applications in RFC 821. SMTP defines a set of rules for exchanging email between computers. The email framework based on SMTP assumes that there exists an underlying trust between sender and receiver and hence, when sender and receiver transfer email, their default behavior is to accept each other's representations. Spammers exploit this factor to target the recipients.

To deal with spammers threats, different types of technological solutions are proposed. These mechanisms can be implemented by individual users, Internet Service Providers (ISPs) and by various third parties. These filtering techniques can work on server and/or client side. Server side spam filtering solutions offers reduction in network load, reduction in computational complexity at client side and ease of collaborative filtering; but can lead to delete legitimate e-mails by incorrectly labeling them as spam. Also they do not eliminate bandwidth overload since they work at the recipient side. In contrast, client side spam filtering solutions offers more personalized spam management and no need of dedicated mail servers.

Further, these methods can include filtering, blocking and hiding methods. Filtering can be carried out by the end users, ISPs or proxy servers to simply ignore unwanted messages. Blocking can be carried out by the end users, ISPs or proxy servers to refuse delivery of spam based on the databases consisting blacklisted host addresses that are used frequently by spammers. Hiding involves concealment of e-mail addresses by the recipients from spammers. Further, mail clients can be configured not to automatically download or display HTML, images or attachments by default.

Some spam filters use network information like IP address or email address of known or suspected spammers, which is maintained in central repository in the form of black listings or grey listings. Challenge response based spam filtering systems challenge to the sender when the incoming messages are from addresses which are not on the white list. In this case, senders are forced to prove their identity first.

The methods which are based on white listings may not be effective and time consuming in case of large organizations having large sized white listings. At the same time these techniques assumes safely that the email addresses in white listings will not send any spam, which may not be true always. Spammers can compromise these servers using viruses/Trojans and force them to send spam from white listings. To reduce false positive rate, some spam filters reject the email from unknown sender for first time. Generally, spammers will not try to send again to the email ids which have been failed in very first place, but real servers will. If spam filters receive the message next time from the same email id, then this email address will be marked safe. This may delay in processing legitimate mails from unknown senders and consume more bandwidth due to resending task (Sanz, HidalgoGomez, & PérezCortizo, 2008).

To deal with compromised senders sending spam, senders can be challenged using Completely Automated Public Turing test to tell Computers and Humans Apart (CAPTCHA) methods which enforce the sending entity to prove as human, before sending bulk mails (CAPTCHA, 2000). A CAPTCHA is an image that contains a word or letters and numbers that have been warped in a way that makes image analysis difficult and, allegedly, deciphering by humans easy. We know that, Google offers "reCAPTCHA Mailhide", a free web service which allows user to protect their email address from spammers. Once user register his email address with this web service, it provides user an URL and HTML code for the protected email address which user can share with his contacts. When clicked on this URL, the recipient will be challenged using CAPTCHA in order to view the protected email address. However, this protection method may affect the usability of website. Visitors with poor vision or are color blind may have difficulty identifying CAPTCHA letters. Blind visitors using screen readers will be blocked from accessing the site.

Further, honeypot programs can also be used in order to discover spam activities and protect real servers from spam attacks. Some filters inspect the email content for certain words, phrases or patterns that indicates spam (Maria and Yiu-Kai, 2009). In case the email is classified as spam, the reputation parameter associated with that sender can be decreased. Once this parameter value crosses some threshold, the sender email id is marked in black listings. Spammers can easily get evaded from static rule based spam filtering methods using simple word obfuscation techniques. Also, legitimate messages containing any of these forbidden words may get blocked by these filters. Statistical detection techniques are based on machine learning methods like Naive Bayes (NB), K-nearest neighbor (K-NN), support vector machines (SVMs) etc. performs better due to their continuous learning ability. Some shaping filters are employed to make sending high volumes of email traffic to be more expensive to prevent spammers from sending bulk mails. They may delay the receipt of mail from unknown senders.

As internet is open to both the legitimate as well as the spammers, it is impossible to stop the activities of the spammers completely. Blocking e-mail traffic from a spam-friendly site often means blocking a great deal of legitimate e-mail. Further modern anti-spam technology is expensive. Due to no strict laws in place, there exist lack of transparency and accountability; as a result spammers continue to act with impunity. Sharing the judgments on probable spam with other users by clients or servers in case of collaborative filtering environment, also may not work as message marked as spam for some client may not be for other client.

In reality, there exists no anti-spam technique which can provide a complete solution to the spam problem. By placing the strict laws and efficient technical methods spammers activities can be curtailed to a great extent.

1.5.3. Legal Methods (Jacob, 2004)

In the absence of adequate technological protection, stringent uniform global legislation is essential to deal with spam. The first national anti-spam bill CAN-SPAM (Controlling the Assault of Non-Solicited Pornography and Marketing) Act, was introduced in 2003 in the United States Congress, to deal with the spam. Many countries including the European Union, Australia, Netherlands, Italy, Germany, France, Sweden, New Zealand, UK, Austria, Belgium, Estonia also endorsed anti-spam legislation. Australia has the most stringent spam laws under which spammers may be fined up to $1.1 million a day. Instead of prohibiting spammers, some legislation introduced an opt-out procedure wherein senders may communicate with anyone except those who have explicitly opted out. The opt-out method is considered as the weaker method. Some legislation was proposed to restrict the e-mail addresses harvesting from domain name registration records. Several jurisdictions provide for criminal penalties or other governmental enforcement mechanisms in addition to or in place of private actions.

1.6. SPAM FILTERS: MACHINE LEARNING TECHNIQUES

Existing email spam filters are based on either knowledge engineering or machine learning approach. Knowledge engineering approach needs a set of rules to be specified by system administrator. These rules must be updated and maintained frequently, as spammers can easily find the ways to easily escape from such static rules. Machine learning approach needs a set of pre- classified training samples to learn the classification rules. Due to flexibility, machine learning approaches including naïve Bayesian (NB) classifier, the k Nearest Neighbor (k-NN) classifier, the neural network (NN) classifier and support vector machine (SVM) classifier have been widely used for spam detection.

Generally, the spam classifiers are trained using set of messages belonging to both spam S and legitimate L classes (see Figure 4 (a)). During testing phase, the labeled test messages are exposed to the filter for classification (see Figure 4 (b)). By computing the degree of misclassification of the classifier output, one can evaluate its performance. The test dataset is similar but disjoint of the training set.

Here, we will quickly review following classifiers.

Figure 4. Spam Filter

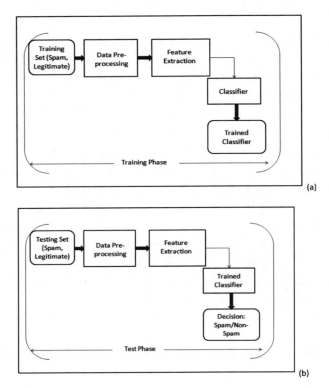

(a)

(b)

1.6.1. The Naive Bayesian Classifier

If $P(x \mid c)$ is the probability of obtaining a message x from class $c \subset (S, L)$, where class c can be Spam (S) or Legitimate (L) then the Bayes' rule is given as in equation (1).

$$P(c \mid x) = \frac{P(x \mid c)P(c)}{P(x)} \tag{1}$$

where, $P(x)$ denotes the a-priori probability of message x, $P(c)$ is the apriori probability of class c and $P(c \mid x)$ is the a-posteriori probability of determining class c of given unknown message x. If $P(S \mid x) > P(L \mid x)$, classify x as spam, otherwise classify it as legitimate mail. In Bayesian classifier, $P(x \mid c)$ and $P(c)$ for any x are estimated from the training samples.

In general, the message $x = (x_1, x_2, ..., x_m)$ is represented by a feature vector containing many attributes where x_i is equal to 1 if the word w_i is present in the message, and 0 otherwise. Assuming components of the vector x are independent in each class, $P(x \mid c) = \prod_{i=1}^{m} P(x_i \mid c)$ is calculated. Either all or most relevant words that are present in the training messages are selected for determining the attributes of the feature vector.

1.6.2. k-Nearest Neighbors (k-NN) Classifier

K-NN classifier is a simplest non-parametric method which can be used for both classification and regression tasks. In k-NN classifier, the distances of message x to all training messages are calculated to find the k nearest neighbors. Here, k is user defined positive integer, typically small that decides the number of nearest neighbors required in the classification. If one or more messages among the k nearest neighbors of x are spam, then classify x as spam, otherwise classify it as legitimate mail. Hence, x is classified by a majority vote of its neighbors and x is assigned to the class which is most common among its k nearest neighbors as shown in Figure 5. The unlabeled sample here will be classified as Group1, when $k = 3$ is set.

Figure 5. k-NN Classification example

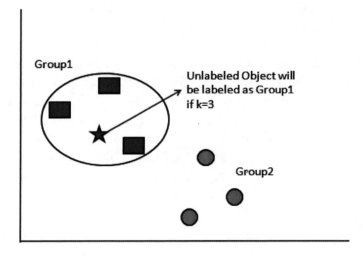

The common weighting scheme consists in giving each neighbor a weight of $\frac{1}{d}$, where d can be the Hamming or Euclidean distance to the neighbor. The high degree of local sensitivity makes k-NN classifier highly susceptible to noise in the training data. In general, a higher value of k results in a smoother, less locally sensitive, function.

1.6.3. Neural Networks (NN) Classifier

Neural Network can be viewed as certain complex function that may be decomposed into smaller parts (neurons, processing units) and represented graphically as a network of these neurons. Two classical kinds of NN are perceptron and the multilayer perceptron which are used generally.

Perceptron is based on finding a linear function of the feature vector $f(x) = w^T x + b$ such that $f(x) > 0$ for vectors of one class, and $f(x) < 0$ for vectors of other class. Here $w = (w_1, w_2, ..., w_m)$ is the vector of coefficients (weights) of the function, and b is the bias. If the vectors to be classified have only two components $c \subset (S, L)$, they can be represented as points on a plane. The decision function of a perceptron can be represented as a line that divides the plane in two parts. Vectors in one half-plane will be classified as belonging to one class, vectors in the other half-plane—as belonging to the other class.

During perceptron learning phase, initial values of w and b are chosen arbitrarily (w0, b0) of the decision function and updates them iteratively. The algorithm stops when a decision function is found that correctly classifies all the training samples. If the classes are not linearly separable, then the learning algorithm will never converge.

Multilayer perceptron is a nonlinear classifier function that may be visualized as a network with several layers of neurons, connected in a feed forward manner. The neurons in the first layer are called input neurons, and represent input variables. The neurons in the last layer are called output neurons and provide function result value. The layers between the first and the last are called hidden layers. Each neuron in the network is similar to a perceptron. During training phase, weights and biases of all the neurons are calculated for which the network will have as small error on the training set as possible.

1.6.4. Support Vector Machine (SVM) Classifier

Support Vector Machines (SVM) is most widely used machine learning techniques a family of algorithms which is developed by V. Vapnik, which is based on finding a linear separation boundary $w^T x + b = 0$ that correctly classifies training samples. The maximal margin separating hyperplane for a training set X is determined. During classification, the class of any message x is determined by finding the *sign* $(w^T x + b)$.

These classifier may adopt different learning modes like supervised (where all training data set is labeled), semi-supervised (where part of training data set is labeled), unsupervised (also called clustering where the training data set is unlabeled) and active (which allows classifier to get label for some unlabeled training data set from user), online and incremental learning.

1.7. EVALUATION METRICS FOR SPAM FILTERS

Let, spam represents positive class and legitimate as negative class, in case of spam filtering problem. Then, TP, FP, TN and FN denote true positive, false positive, true negative and true positive decisions respectively in case of any classifier output decision as shown in Table 1. Table 1 shows the relationship between predicted classifier output and the actual labeled or correct output.

Besides accuracy, other parameters recall and precision of classifier is also stated as evaluation parameters. Recall is the fraction of messages assigned to a category by the classifier as in Equation 1.1 while precision is the fraction of correctly assigned messages to a category as in Equation 1.2. Another measure F1 gives equal importance to both recall and precision of classifier and is given as in Equation 1.3.

Table 1. Confusion Matrix

		Actual	
		Spam (+ve)	Legitimate(-ve)
Predicted	Spam (+ve)	TP	FP
	Legitimate(-ve)	FN	TN

$$\mathrm{Re}\,call = \frac{TP}{TP + FN} \qquad (1.1)$$

$$\mathrm{Pr}\,ecision = \frac{TP}{TP + FP} \qquad (1.2)$$

$$F1 = \frac{2 \times \mathrm{Re}\,call \times \mathrm{Pr}\,ecision}{\mathrm{Re}\,call + \mathrm{Pr}\,ecision} \qquad (1.3)$$

The error of classification legitimate message as spam represents false positive (FP) condition which cannot be afforded by any user. Classification of spam message as legitimate message represents false negative (FN) condition which can be tolerated compared to the FP condition. Hence while evaluating spam filters, the asymmetry of costs associated to these misclassifications need to be considered.

The parameters False Positive Rate (FPR) and True Positive Rate (TPR), are defined as in Equation 1.4 and Equation 5 respectively. TPR is equivalent to the Recall of positive class.

$$FPR = \frac{FP}{FP + TN} \qquad (1.4)$$

$$TPR = \frac{TP}{TP + FN} \qquad (1.5)$$

Based on type of output required, these filters can be configured as 1) hard classifier with only two outputs – spam or non-spam or 2) soft classifier with indication that how likely a message to be spam on continuous scale (Let us say, 1=sure spam and 0=sure non-spam) or ordinal scale (categories like…, sure spam, likely spam, unsure, likely non-spam, sure non-spam).

The filter can be configured to process one message or several messages at a time. The classification task or updating classifiers memory can be done automatically at specified intervals or it can be initiated by client. Although, most of the existing spam filters are based on supervised learning, they can also be configured to adopt real time active learning, where a client is asked to mark a message and the result is used to update classifiers memory. Unsupervised learning or clustering may be used to find groups of similar messages.

1.8. LAWS AND REGULATIONS AGAINST SPAMMERS

Large number of anti-spam legislations passed and the severe punishments meted out to spammers are indicative of the fact that, the international community has recognized the spam menace and is taking steps to combat it effectively. Details of some of the anti-spam laws of various countries (The Center for Internet and Society, 2015) are given in Table 2. Due to non-uniform global legislation against spam, it is difficult to apply effective legal measures against spam. Here, anonymous natured internet spams are not captured in the frame of the nations boundaries.

The countries like United States of America and Singapore has opted the spam regulation model in which messages may be sent to any recipients at all times until the recipient voluntarily unsubscribe such services. As the default the model presumes the right to market, the burden of reduction of spam will be kept on the recipients (The Center for Internet and Society, 2015). There is no guarantee that the 'unsubscribe' link provided will be genuine. In contrast the countries like Canada, Australia and the United Kingdom has opted a spam regulation model where the messages may be sent to recipients only when they voluntarily share their contact details to subscribe such messages. This model causes reduction in commercial or spam messages drastically (The Center for Internet and Society, 2015).

1.9. THREAT LEVEL: TEXT SPAM AND IMAGE SPAM

A number of inbuilt e-mail filtering software associated with every e-mail service provider; broadly categorize the spam mails into text spam and image spam. To handle text spam, text categorization techniques are used, in which the email messages acts as document and classified into the classes spam and legitimate email.

Table 2. Country and Related Laws/Act

Country	Legislation
Australia	Spam Act 2003
Argentina	Personal Data Protection Act (2000)
Austria	Austrian Telecommunications Act 1997
Belgium	Law of March 11 2003
Brazil	None (loosely; MovimentoBrasileiro de Combateao Spam)
Canada	Canada's Anti-Spam Legislation 2014 (CASL)
China	Regulations on Internet email Services
Cyprus	Regulation of Electronic Communications and Postal Services Law of 2004
Czech Republic	Act No. 480/2004 Coll., on Certain Information Society Services
Denmark	Danish marketing practices act
European Union	Directive on Privacy and Electronic Communications
Finland	Act on Data Protection in Electronic Communications (516/2004)
France	Law of June 21 2004 for confidence in the digital economy
Germany	Act against Unfair Competition
Hong Kong	Unsolicited Electronic Messaging Ordinance
Hungary	Act CVIII of 2001 on Electronic Commerce
India	None (loosely; Information Technology Act, 2000)
Indonesia	Undang-undangInformasidanTransaksiElektronic (ITE) (Internet Law)
Ireland	European Communities (Electronic Communications Networks and Services) (Data Protection and Privacy) Regulations 2003
Israel	Communications Law (Telecommunications and Broadcasting), 1982
Italy	Data Protection Code (Legislative Decree no. 196/2003)
Japan	The Law on Regulation of Transmission of Specified Electronic Mail
Malaysia	Communications and Multimedia Act 1998
Malta	Data Protection Act (CAP 440)
Netherlands	Dutch Telecommunications Act
New Zealand	Unsolicited Electronic Messages Act 2007
Pakistan	Prevention of Electronic Crimes Ordinance 2007
Russia	None (loosely: Russian Civil Code: Art.309)
Singapore	Spam Control Act 2007
South Africa	Electronic Communications and Transactions Act, 2002, & Consumer Protection Act, 2008
South Korea	Act on Promotion of Information and Communication and Communications Network Utilization and Information Protection of 2001
Spain	Act 34/2002 of 11 July on Information Society Services and Electronic Commerce
Sweden	Marknadsföringslagen (1995:450)"Swedish Marketing Act"
Turkey	ElektronikTicaretinDüzenlenmesiHakkındaKanun "Act About Regulation of E-Commerce"
United Kingdom	Privacy and Electronic Communications (EC Directive) Regulations 2003
United States	Controlling the Assault of Non-Solicited Pornography and Marketing Act of 2003 (CAN-SPAM Act of 2003)

1.9.1. Text Spam

Text Spam is similar to the normal mails in which the relevant text is inserted into the body of the mail by the spammers as shown in Figure 6 (Metsis, Androutsopoulos, & Paliouras, 2006). These are easy to fabricate and does not require any sophisticated training to train the spammers for designing the spam. Text spam are easy to filter out by traditional text-based methods (like Radical Spam, Bog filter, Spam Bayes). The words or text present in the body of the mail are extracted with the help of Optical Character Recognition (OCR) and these words or text are used to decide whether a mail is spam or not. These texts based spam are of two types:

1. **Keyword Based Text Spam (Sanz, HidalgoGomez, & PerezCortizo, 2008):** In this type of spam, keywords related to banking, sports, sexual and other fields are available in the body of the mail. These keywords which are frequently available in the spam make the mail as spam or ham. Anti-spammers make use of these keywords to decide whether a mail is spam or not.
2. **Text Based Text Spam (Chang, & Lin, 2011):** In this type of spam, in place of keywords, texts related to banking, sports, sexual and other fields are available in the body of the mail. These texts which are frequently available in the spam make the mail as spam or ham. Anti-spammers make use of these texts to decide whether a mail is spam or not.

1.9.2. Image Spam

In order to evade from text spam detection techniques, spammers came out with the concept of the image spam (Krasser et al., 2007; Biggio et al., 2007). Here, the spammers embed the required text so that they can overcome the text based spam filters as shown in Figure 7. Image spam utilizes more network resources than text spam due to their large size. Image-based spam is becoming a new threat to the Internet and its users. These are costly in nature and sophisticated training is imparted to the spammers for designing the spam.

Figure 6. Example of Text spam

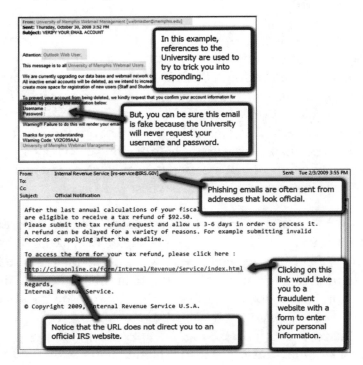

1.9.3. Comparison of Text and Image Spam

Both text and image spam produces negative effects and results in the loss of efficient resources however both have different radius of effect. Image spam incur more ill effects as compared to text spam. A comparison of both is given in Table 3.

Image spam poses a great threat to email clients due to its adverse effects on storage, bandwidth and processing requirements. According to McAfee (Frank, 2007) image spam constituted 65% of all the spam emails, by the end of 2006.

Figure 7. Example of image spam

Table 3. Comparison: Text and Image Spam

Text Spam	Image Spam
Easy to fabricate	Difficult to fabricate
Less costly	More costly
Less complicated	More complicated
Less adverse effect on bandwidth	More adverse effect on bandwidth
Anti-spam filters can be made with simple and less costly techniques such as OCR.	Anti-spam filters are made of complex and costly techniques such as Wavelets, Decision tree etc.
Less sever effect on internet hardware resources.	More sever effect on internet hardware resources.
Less processing is done in ant-spam filters.	More processing is done in ant-spam filters.

1.10. IMAGE FILE FORMATS

Some of the most popular image and file formats are as;

- **Tagged Image File Format (TIFF):** This highly flexible platform independent file format is designed for raster data interchange. Theoretically, TIFF can support imagery with multiple bands (up to 64K bands), arbitrary number of bits per pixel, data cubes, and multiple images per file, including thumbnail sub-sampled images. Supported color spaces include gray-scale, pseudo-color (any size), RGB, YCbCr, CMYK, and CIELab. TIFF supports the following compression types: raw uncompressed, PackBits, Lempel-Ziv-Welch (LZW), CCITT Fax 3 and 4, JPEG; and pixel formats: 1-64 bit integer, 32 or 64 bit IEEE floating point.
- **Bitmap (BMP):** BMP, a raster image format files are stored in a device-independent bitmap (DIB) format that allows the operating system to display the bitmap on any type of display device. Windows versions 3.0 and later support run-length encoded (RLE) formats for compressing bitmaps that use 4 or 8 bits per pixel. This compression comes at the expense of the color variety and depth.
- **Joint Photographic Experts Group (JPEG):** This lossy image compression standard compresses the image file size at the cost of image quality to considerably shrink the file size. JPEG works well on photographs, naturalistic artwork, and similar material. It exploits the fact that human eyes perceive small color changes less accurately than small changes in brightness.
- **Graphic Interchange Format (GIF):** GIF is adopted by the World Wide Web for its efficiency and widespread familiarity. GIF files are limited to 8-bit color palettes supporting no more than 256 colors. The GIF format incorporates a compression scheme to keep file sizes at a minimum. GIF works for images of text and diagrams better than for real-world images.
- **Portable Network Graphics (PNG):** For the Web, PNG really has three main advantages over GIF: alpha channels (variable transparency), gamma correction (cross-platform control of image brightness), and two-dimensional interlacing (a method of progressive display). PNG provides a lossless compression and supports only a single image per file.

1.11. SUMMARY

In recent decades, there has been incredible growth in the usage of various internet applications by users. E-mail is one of the low-cost, efficient and convenient means of internet applications that supports distant communication. However, according to a report released by Kaspersky Lab, in the six years from 2001 to 2007, the percentage of spam mail increased from 5% to 95% (Peng, & Uehara, 2011).

This chapter has revealed the secrets and tricks of spammers to evade from anti-spam techniques. Day by day, spammer are trying their hard efforts to make spam contents visible to the end user; while at the same time, they are trying all tricks to make the spam content undetected by spam filters. The chapter also states various techniques to handle spam along with the corresponding existing laws/regulations. Although, technology and law together play a crucial role against spam, there is no silver bullet that will solve the spam problem.

Finally, this chapter has exposed the dark side of image spam. Compared to text spam, image spam poses a great threat to email clients due to its adverse effects on storage, bandwidth and processing requirements. This shows a need for necessary call to action against the spam images.

REFERENCES

Absolute Astronomy. (2016). *E-mail spam*. Available from: http://www.absoluteastronomy.com/topics/E-mail_spam

Biggio, B., Fumera, G., Pillai, I., & Roli, F. (2007). Image Spam Filtering using Visual Information. *Proceedings of 14th International Conference on Image Analysis and Processing*, 105-110. doi:10.1109/ICIAP.2007.4362765

CAPTCHA. (2000). *The CAPTCHA Project*. Available from: http://captcha.net

Chang, C., & Lin, C. (2011). LibSVM: A Library for Support Vector Machines. *ACM Transactions on Intelligent Systems and Technology*, 2(3), 1–27. doi:10.1145/1961189.1961199

COMMTOUCH. (2013). *Internet Threats Trends Report –October 2013*. Available from: http://www.commtouch.com/uploads/pdf/Commtouch-Internet-Threats-Trend-Report-Q3-2013.pdf

Dynamic Web Solutions. (2016). *Unwanted Email or Spam: Internet "Junk Mail"*. Available from: http://dynamicwebs.com.au/tutorials/spam.htm

Frank, W. J. (2007). *No slowing growth of image spam in 2006*. Available from: https://www.scmagazineuk.com/no-slowing-growth-of-image-spam-in-2006/article/563174/

Goodman, J., Cormack, G., & Heckerman, D. (2007). Spam and the Ongoing Battle for The Inbox. *Communications of the ACM*, *50*(2), 24–33. doi:10.1145/1216016.1216017

Jacob, S. (2004). The Role of Public Policy in the Fight against Spam. *Journal of Engineering and Public Policy*, *8*. Available from: http://www.wise-intern. org/journal/2004/WISE2004-JacobScottFinalPaper.pdf

Krasser, S., Yuchun, T., Gould, J., Alperovitch, D., & Judge, P. (2007). Identifying Image Spam Based on Header and File Properties using C4.5 Decision Trees and Support Vector Machine Learning. Proceedings of Information Assurance and Security Workshop (IAW-2007), 255-261.

MAAWG Organization. (2011). *Email Metrics Program: The Network Operators' Perspective*. Available from: https://www.m3aawg.org/sites/ default/files/document/MAAWG_2011_Q1-4_Metrics_Report15Rev.pdf

Maria, S. P., & Yiu-Kai, N. (2009). SpamED: A Spam E-Mail Detection Approach Based on Phrase Similarity. *Journal of the American Society for Information Science and Technology*, *60*(2), 393–409. doi:10.1002/asi.20962

Metsis, V., Androutsopoulos, I., & Paliouras, G. (2006). Spam Filtering with Naive Bayes - Which Naive Bayes?. *Proceedings of the 3rd Conference on Email and Anti-Spam (CEAS-2006)*.

Peng, W., & Uehara, M. (2011). Using Diagonal and Horizontal Vertical Sobel Operators Spam Detection. *Proceedings of Third International Conference on Intelligent Networking and Collaborative Systems (INCoS-2011)*, 396–400.

Rahul, D. (2016). Spam: Is it time to legislate? *Legal Services India*. Available from: http://www.legalservicesindia.com/articles/spamli.htm

Sanz, E. P., Hidalgomez, J. M., & Perezcortizo, J. C. (2008). *Email Spam Filtering. In Advances in Computers* (Vol. 74, pp. 45–114). Elsevier.

Stretfeld, D. (2003). Opening Pandora's In-Box. *Los Angeles Times*. Available from: http://articles.latimes.com/2003/may/11/business/fi-spam11

Symantec. (2014). *Symantec Report.* Available from: http://www.symantec.com/securityresponse/landing/spam/

The Center for Internet and Society. (2015). *Anti-Spam Laws in Different Jurisdictions: A Comparative Analysis.* Available from: https://www.google.co.in/url?sa=t&rct=j&q=&esrc=s&source=web&cd=3&cad=rja&uact=8&ved=0ahUKEwi-qdHgg8fRAhXEt48KHUIBBnMQFggpMAI&url=http%3A%2F%2Fcis-india.org%2Finternet-governance%2Fblog%2Fanti-spam-laws-in-different-jurisdictions&usg=AFQjCNHqT3PdgewoTupgPMUMXnucxW3YUQ

Chapter 2
Image Spam:
Characteristics and Generation

ABSTRACT

Each and everything in this world have some sort of unique and special characteristics associated with it. These characteristics aid us to differentiate among various things. Similarly the spam mails exhibit some special characteristics by which they can easily be distinguished from genuine mails. In order to understand the characteristic of Image spam, it is important to have an overview of the characteristics of the spam emails in general. The good understanding of these characteristics will offer the sufficient knowledge for anti-spammers during the development of anti-spam frameworks for both server and client end.

2.1. SPAM EMAIL: PRELIMINARY ANALYSIS

In general, spam mails show evidence of following important properties, which would raise the suspicion in the minds of anti spam analysts (POLICYPATROL, 2016; Ward and Aiko, 2010).

1. **Presence of Some Code or Text Outside HTML Tags:** Generally in any legitimate html content, there exists no code or text outside the HTML tags. However, in case of some spam mails, some code or text is written outside the HTML tags to hide it from the recipient. So these

DOI: 10.4018/978-1-68318-013-5.ch002

types of emails should be dealt with rigorous analysis in order to trace the origin of such mails and to block them at the server side itself.

2. **Presence of Some Text in Messages Containing Images:** Most of the spam filters blocks messages containing only images and no text at all. To evade from such spam filters, spammers will add some text in the messages, like simple '.' or any other character in very small font, which may not be noticeable easily by recipient.

3. **Presence of Recipients Identity in Subject Field:** To trick the recipient, spammer will try to personalize the message by adding recipients identity like name/email id in the subject field of mail.

4. **Presence of Encoded Message Header and Body:** To evade from spam filters, spammers encode message header and body using base64 encoding and make the content unreadable for spam filters. Many email clients support base64 decoding by default.

5. **Presence of Some Sequence in Sender Address Field:** Spammers register thousands of automated generated email ids which are further used to send the spam messages. These email ids are generated in volume by spammers by just adding some number or text sequences with the help of automated programs.

6. **Addresses Mentioned in "From: and Reply To:" Fields do not Match:** Although this common feature appears in most of the spam mails, these types of emails should be dealt with rigorous analysis as the same feature can also be present in the legitimate emails too. Hence, there is a need to carry out a thorough investigation before blocking any origin otherwise it can lead to blocking of the legitimate emails.

7. **Presence of Image:** Spammers can easily escape from word filters, by including an image in spam messages. In addition, upon opening the email message, the image is downloaded to client machine from the spammer's website. Since each message contains a unique ID, the spammer will know exactly which recipient has viewed the mail. This indicates spammers the email addresses which are 'live' so that more spam mails can be sent to these addresses by spammers. The spammers build the database of these live email addresses. They even share and sell these databases with other marketing companies for financial benefits.

8. **Hiding Recipient's Email Address in Other Fields:** Generally, most professional companies do not prefer this method for sending newsletters or mailings. However, spammers may hide the recipient's email address

in the "Bcc:" field or X-receiver field instead of writing in the "To: or Cc:" fields, along with a substantial number of other email addresses. Indirectly, spammers conceal the fact from the recipient that the mail was sent in bulk to many other recipients. The email list of these other recipients is also hidden from main recipient. Blocking such emails without a local recipient in the "To: or Cc:" field, will block all bcc: messages, including legitimate mailings also.

9. **Presence of HTML Content:** HTML messages usually include a plain text version of the email. This makes any email recipients including email clients that cannot read HTML to view the message in plain text format. However, many spammers tend to send HTML messages without this plain text body part in order to reduce the message size and force recipients to read the HTML version (Ward and Aiko, 2010). When such spam messages are opened, the HTML body automatically opens an image and connects to a web site. However, some newsletters also tend to send messages without a plain text body part; hence it is important to use a white list of allowed newsletters so as not to catch any false positives.

10. **Presence of HTML Tags:** Some spammers try to circumvent content filters by placing lots of HTML comment tags within the email body text (Ward and Aiko, 2010). Spammers use HTML tags to split words. In this way, content filters will not recognize the spam words since they are separated by comment tags. The recipient however, will not see the comment tags since these are not displayed when viewing the message in HTML. Therefore it is important to use an email filter that can filter emails by removing HTML tags first.

11. **Presence of Scripts:** Some spammers place entire message inside scripts (like, java scripts) in order to circumvent content filters. The text of the message will appear, whenever the recipient email client software executes these scripts. Script is usually hidden inside an HTML comment block and most of the filters ignore HTML comments. Since legitimate email message mostly do not contain scripts, it is easy to classify such emails as spam.

Existence of above properties can be considered during analysis using simple weightage parameter and if the value exceeds some threshold, the mail can be marked as spam. Figure 1 shows a sample spam email captured by rediffmail account and Figure 2 shows the header information for the same spam. Here we can see, the various text components which can be verified

Image Spam

Figure 1. Sample Spam Email

Figure 2. Header Information of Sample Spam email

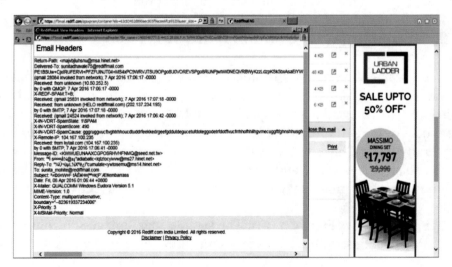

are From:, To:, Subject, Headers and actual text contents. These fields can be analyzed by any text based email spam filters.

2.2. CHARACTERISTICS OF IMAGE SPAM

Similar to the theory based on classic battle of virus and antivirus industry, spammers explore new technologies in an effort to keep one step ahead of spam filters. Image spam is one of the latest obfuscating technique developed by spammers to bypass conventional text based spam filters. In image spam, the content of the spam message is in the form of an embedded image. As the body of image spam contains no text, the conventional text based spam filters therefore fails to notice it. Moreover, the image spam can be more fascinating and convincing than text alone. Image spam is reported accounting for roughly 40 percent of all spam traffic now, and is still on the rise. This rising threats in turn have turned the attention of researchers and software security providers to investigate more constructive technologies to filter image spam. Following are few important characteristics exhibited by image spam and hence these features will be useful to detect them.

2.2.1. Spam Images Contain More Text Area

The major intention of any spammer is to convey the information (which he desire) to the recipients of the emails; generally for advertisement or marketing purpose. To achieve this goal, spammer embeds the text in the image. These texts occupy the certain amount of image area, which is known as the text area. Generally the text area available in the legitimate image is less as compared to the spam image (Hsia and Chen, 2009). Figure 3 (a)-(c), shows sample spam image, legitimate image without and with text respectively.

1.   **Spam Image (Figure 3 (a)):** The sample spam image shown in Figure 3(a) contains the text which is embedded by the spammer. The text area is indicated in the red color rectangle. This text area is nearly 50% of the total area and hence the amount of area covered by the text can be considered as one of the characteristic to identify the spam images.

Figure 3. Sample Images attached with emails

(a) Sample Spam Image

(b) Sample Legitimate Image without Text

(c) Legitimate image with Text

So techniques which utilize this characteristic can be developed and a threshold value to the text area can be set in these techniques for classification. If the text area is more than the threshold value than the image will be considered as spam otherwise as legitimate.

2. **Legitimate image without Text (Figure 3 (b)):** The sample spam image shown in Figure 3(b) is a legitimate image which does not have

any text embedded in it. It does not convey any specific meaning such as marketing of some specific brand of mobile, clothing etc. Hence, it is clear that in any case the text is a specific ingredient in spam images where as these are generally unavailable in legitimate images.

3. **Legitimate image with Text (Figure 3 (c)):** The sample spam image shown in Figure 3(c) is a legitimate image representing sign board with some text. In many such natural or legitimate images, we find text embedded. However, the size of this text area is very small and covers little space in the image. So threshold can be set to distinguish the anti spam techniques after analyzing such types of the natural images.

From above sample images, one can conclude that the spam images contain more text as compared to that of legitimate images. Hence, the threshold based detectors can be designed based on text area characteristics like; if the text area is more than the predetermined threshold value then the image can be considered as spam.

2.2.2. Colour Saturation

Colour saturation is quantified as the fraction of the total number of pixels in the image for which the difference max(R, G, B) – min(R, G, B) is greater. Presence of synthetic graphics and sharp or clear objects makes spam images more saturated compared to natural scene images. However, the spam images are less saturated compared to generic legitimate computer-generated graphics images (Wang et al. 2010; Dredze, Gevaryahu, and Elias, 2007). The saturation of a color depends on both light intensity and its distribution across the spectrum of different wavelengths. The purest/most saturated color is achieved by using just one wavelength at a high intensity, such as in laser light. If the intensity drops, then as a result the saturation drops. To de-saturate a color of given intensity, one can add colors like white, black, gray etc. This can be easily understood by the Figure 4 (a) and (b).

1. **Original image (Figure 4 (a)):** In this original image the area inside the circle and the shade indicated by the dashed line are darker. This indicates that the image consists of less number of pixels for which difference max(R, G, B) – min(R, G, B) is low.

2. **Spam image (Figure 4 (b)):** In this spam image the value of the Croma component increased by 50% due to which the darker portions of the original images are becoming much brighter. This is due to the

Figure 4. (a) Original image and (b) Spam Image Croma component increased by 50%

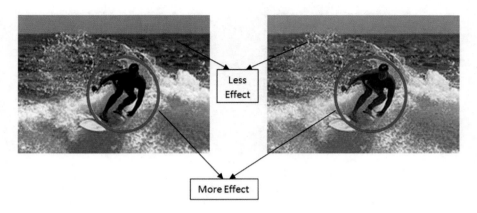

manipulation carried out in the Croma value present in the pixel values. As a result of this the image is now having more number of pixels for which difference $\max(R, G, B) - \min(R, G, B)$ is more. So it is understood from the above two images that the spam image is having more color saturation as compared to the legitimate image.

2.2.3. Color Heterogeneity Differs in Spam Images

Depending upon the uniformity or non-uniformity in the composition with respect to the attributes like color, shape, size, weight, height, distribution, texture, etc.; we can say that spam images are different than that of natural images. Computer generated spam images contain fewer colours than natural scene images. Natural scene images have vast ranges of different colour. As a result the heterogeneity of spam images is lower ham that of the legitimate image (Byun et al. 2007).

1. **Homogenous Image (Figure 5 (a)):** As it can be clearly seen and understood that the Pixels values in the image is not changing drastically and are closely associated with the other pixel values. Such types of images in which pixels values are uniform are generally natural or ham images.

2. **Heterogeneity Image (Figure 5 (b)):** As it can be clearly seen and understood that the Pixels values in the image are changing drastically and not are closely associated with the other pixel values. There exists no relation among the pixel values. Such types of images in which

Figure 5. (a) Homogeneous Image and (b) Heterogeneous Image

pixels values are non-uniform are generally computer generated or spam images. The drastic changes in the pixel values or heterogeneity is shown in the red circles for easy understanding. The pixel values are changing to uniform color to red and yellow in the image.

2.2.4. Presence of Obfuscating Techniques

Early Anti spam techniques were signature based or utilizes the OCR techniques to detect the spam images. So in order to defeat these Spammers uses various obfuscating techniques such as character breaking, distortion of words, merging (parametric complexity), rotation, scaling, translation etc or introducing the noise in the image text region etc. The presence of any obfuscating techniques used in an image indicates that an image is likely to be spam. Although these features were not capable of detecting the spams images independently but are good means of discriminating the low level characteristic of text which are embedded into the image (Biggio et al. 2007; Zuo et al. 2009a; Zuo Li, et al. 2009b).

1. **Character Breaking (Figure 6 (a))**: As shown in the Figure 8, the character breaking in the words is carried out by the spammers to avoid detection or extraction of these words from the images by the OCR based spam detection techniques.
2. **Distortion of Words (Figure 6 (b))**: Spammers carries out the distortion of the words as shown in Figure 9, which makes OCR based spam

Figure 6. Obfuscation techniques on images

detection techniques to treat it as an image instead of the words and hence indirectly to escape from detection by reducing efficiency of the detection.

3. **Merging of Words (Figure 6 (c)):** Words are merged into one another due to which they form different types of the shapes and hence, OCR based spam detection techniques is not able to detect these shapes.

4. **Scaling of Words (Figure 6 (d)):** Spammers keep on changing the size of the characters and the words in order to defeat the OCR based spam detection techniques.

5. **Rotation of Words (Figure 6 (e)):** The spammers keep on providing some rotation angle to the characters and the words by doing so it looks like some image instead of character to the OCR based spam detection techniques.

6. **Adding of Noise (Figure 6 (f)):** The spammers insert the external noise to the spam images so that the OCR based spam detection techniques could not be able to extract the characters from the images.

2.2.5. Frequency of Words

Generally some specific words are repeated in the spam images which increases the frequency of these words more compared to other words (Harisinghaney at al. 2014). Database of these words can be prepared by extracting them by OCR based spam detection techniques; which is also known as "Bag of Words". Users can define their own "Bag of Words" in order to decide how many and what words he want to consider for detection of the spam images. Some of the examples of "Bag of Words" are as follows.

1.   Viagra, Sex (Only two words).
2.   Liquor, Sale, Free, etc (Any number of words based on user preference)

2.2.6. Nature of Metadata

The parameters like compressibility, file size, file name, and area of ham images are different as compared to the spam images (Uemura, and Tabata, 2008). The file name are same for the similar images, ham image size is generally bigger as compared to the spam image, content of the spam images is smaller than the ham images so the area and the compressibility is going to higher in the spam images.

2.2.7. Distinct Global Features

Color, texture and shape features are different in spam images as compared to the legitimate images (Mehta et al. 2008). The spam images are computer or artificially generated and the objects contained in them are sharper and cleaner as compared to legitimate images as shown in Figure 7 (a)-(b). The features cannot be easily manipulated by the spammers to make their spam images look like a ham image. As the main intent of sending spam images is to obfuscate the spam filter and send it to as many recipients as possible. Hence, they are of small file size and are not very clear and bright.

2.2.8. Low Luminance Value

Luminance parameter characterizes the brightness of an image. The value of luminance in images can be calculated using HSL (Hue, Saturation, and Luminance) model. The Luminance is lower in computer generated spam

Figure 7. Sample natural and spam image

(a) Natural Image	(b) Spam Image

compared to natural ham images (which are taken from camera) (Hazza and Aziz, 2012).

In a gray scale image, the luminance value is the pixel value. In a color image, the luminance value is given by a weighted sum (Louisiana, 2016) as in Equation (2.1).

$$Luminance = 0.27 \times Red + 0.67 \times Green + 0.06 \times Blue \qquad (2.1)$$

The average of luminance for all the pixels in an image is given as in Equation (2.2).

$$Average\ Luminance = Luminance\ of\ all\ pixels/\ Number\ of\ pixels \qquad (2.2)$$

The image shown in Figure 8 (b) is brighter than the image shown in Figure 8 (a) and hence will have more luminance.

2.2.9. Near-Duplicate Detection or Similarity Between Images

Different Spam images are generated from the same templates (common base image) as they are sent to various recipients at the same time. Various spam images are generated by randomization of the objects or contents of these templates as a result a similarity is present among the spam images. This similarity property can be exploited by the classifier for discriminating them from ham. The classifier can be further trained on new data if the spam images are generated from different templates, which is not a frequent phenomenon

Figure 8. Low and high luminance images

| (a) Low Luminance | (b) High Luminance |

as it is resources intensive (Wang et al. 2007; He, Wen and Zheng, 2009; Qu and Zhang, 2009; Zhang et al. 2009).

2.3. HOW IMAGE SPAM ARE GENERATED?

It is important to understand how the spammers generate the image spam. The methods adopted by the spammers to generate the image spam can be divided into two categories. These are as follows.

2.3.1. Manual Generation of Spam

Initially spammers used to generate the spam images by carrying out the manipulation with the help of some operations such as cut, copy, paste, amending, and merging of two or more images. The drawback of these method are as follows

1. **Costly:** The intervention of human being was more to generate the image spam due to which the fabrication cost (wages of human being) of the spam used to be generally very high.
2. **Time Consuming:** It was a time consuming process as it was fully dependent on the human intervention and also the human being used to take more time to generate the spam as compared to automatic generating process.
3. **Easily Detectable:** The traces left due to simple operations such as cut, copy, paste were easily detectable by the anti spam techniques. As

results the spam were frequently generated due to which the processes become more costly and time consuming.

The examples of manually generated images are given in Figure 9 (a)-(b).

2.3.2. Computer/Automatic Generation of Spam

In order to overcome the drawbacks of the manual generation of spam the spammers started generating the spam with the help of the computer and generally known by the name "graphically generated images". The benefits are as follows.

1. **Less Generation Cost:** The human intervention is not at all or very less intervention is required due to which the graphic generated spam are less costly.
2. **Less Generation Time:** The fabrication process is fully machine (computer) dependent due to which it takes less time to generate the spam as compared to manual generating process.
3. **Difficult to Detect:** The low level features of the original images are manipulated to generate spam images due to which simple anti spam techniques (such as OCR) are not able to detect the spam images. In order to detect these spam more sophisticated and costly techniques are required.

Figure 9. Original and modified images

(a) Original Image   (b) Modified Image

2.4. LIMITATIONS OF EXISTING ANTI SPAM METHODS

In image spam, e-mail text message is embedded into the image and sent as attachments, which will be automatically displayed by most e-mail clients. Hence, traditional content filtering techniques which are based on the analysis of plain text in the subject and body fields of e-mails, are ineffective against image spam.

Some commercial spam filters exhibits low flexibility and low generalisation capability in spam detection, as they are based on manually coded rules which are derived from spam e-mail analysis. Such static rules make them ineffective in detecting e-mails similar, but not identical to those used for rules definition. This suggests the use of machine learning approaches in spam detection for achieving automatic construction of classification rules, and higher generalisation capability.

The problem with many email spam filters is that sometimes a valid message may be blocked. Hence automatically blocking/rejecting mail that is classified as spam will not be useful. The detection techniques should allow user to read the spam email or delete the spam email. To ease the user, these messages can be sorted based on the high probability of non-spam email at the top of list, before providing the messages to the user. The detectors should only indicate spam probability or its degree of confidence for the spam message but should not delete them. Further, the eeturn mails in response to user query should be excluded from the analysis.

Conventional anti-spam methods are based on either source inspection or contents inspection. In source inspection based methods, open relay prohibition, blacklist setting and domain checking are commonly used (Peng and Minoru 2012). In contents inspection based methods, the usual approach is to check for keywords. However, spammers can avoid a keyword filter by sending images instead of text. Hence, multimodal input handling approaches are needed which can analyze both text and image features (Zhang et al. 2009).

Further, there is need of very low false alarm rate by these filters, as the loss of regular mail may cause great losses to the user (Hou et al. 2012). The average user can tolerate a certain amount of spam, but cannot tolerate the loss of a small amount of regular mail. This adds to one of the challenges for existing anti spam methods.

The anti spam methods needs to efficiently handle the massive data. Existing methods of image spam detectors often involves a huge computation and hence they must meet higher processing requirements (Hou et al. 2012).

2.5. IMAGE SPAM DATASET FOR EXPERIMENTATION

Although it is difficult to build email corpora due to the private nature of email communications, there exists some freely available datasets for research and experiments on image spam detection.

2.5.1. Hunter Dataset (Gao et al. 2008)

This dataset consists of 928 spam images and 810 natural images. The spam images were collected (received on the mail) by the authors over the spam of six month. These are JPEG images only and do not contain any animated images. Normal images were randomly downloaded from Flickr.com. These are JPEG images only and do not contain any animated images however they contain 20 scanned copies of the images. The spam dataset can be downloaded from the weblink, http://www.cs.northwestern.edu/~yga751/ML/ISH.htm. The sample images for spam and natural images are shown in Figure 10 and Figure 11 respectively.

2.5.2. Princeton Dataset (Princeton, 2007)

The Princeton Spam Image Benchmark contains spam images collected from multiple email accounts.

The benchmark contains 1071 images in 178 groups or batches. Each batch contains at least 2 images in this benchmark. This dataset can be downloaded from the web link, http://www.cs.princeton.edu/cass/spam/spam_bench/. The sample images for spam images are shown in Figure 12 (a)-(h) respectively.

2.5.3. Dredze Dataset (Dredze, Gevaryahu and Elias, 2007)

This dataset consists of 3299 spam images and 2021 natural images. The spam images were collected from the mailbox by the author over the spam of six month. These images contain various formats such as JPEG, PNG, GIF etc of the image. These dataset can be downloaded from the link, https://www.cs.jhu.edu/~mdredze/datasets/image_spam/. The size of Personal Image Spam and Personal Image Ham is 29 MB and 107 MB respectively. The ham/spam dataset is prepared by collecting email data from the mailboxes of two real users and by deleting all images which are considered private. The Spam Archive images were taken from the Spam Archive data provided by Giorgio

Figure 10. Hunter dataset: Sample spam images

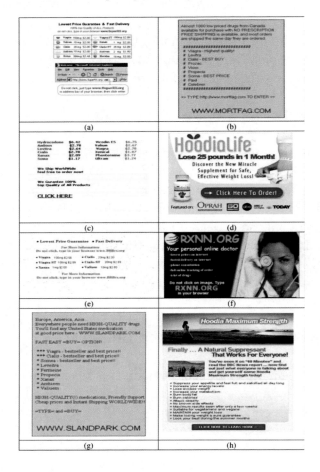

Fumera's group (Giorgio, Pillai and Fabio, 2006). The sample images for spam and natural images are shown in Figure 13 (a)-(h) and Figure 14 (a)-(h) respectively.

The details of the format and the number of the images pertaining to the respected format are shown in Table 1.

2.5.4. SpamArchive (Giorgio, Pillai, Fabio, 2006)

The publicly available SpamArchive corpus (www.spamarchive.org), is a collection of spam e-mails donated by end users for testing, developing, and benchmarking anti-spam tools. A corpus of spam e-mails was collected from October 2004 to August 2005 in the authors' mailboxes using spam e-mails

Figure 11. Hunter dataset: Sample natural images

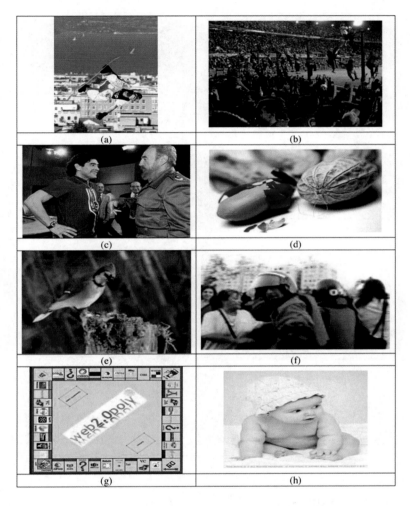

containing attached images. This corpus is made up of around 21,000 spam e-mails, among which around 4% contain attached images with embedded text. The sample images for spam images are shown in Figure 15.

Collection of the legitimate image email corpus is difficult to collect as legitimate emails containing personal information are usually not easy to distribute or legitimate emails containing images are much rarer than spam ones.

Figure 12. Princeton dataset: Sample spam images

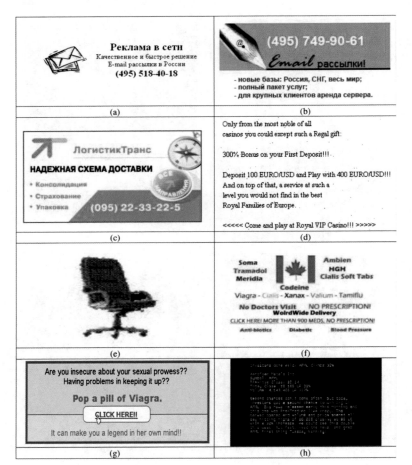

2.5.5. TREC 2007 Spam Corpus (Gordan and Tom, 2007)

The publicly available TREC 2007 spam corpus (Gordan and Tom, 2007) is made up of messages collected in 2007 from different accounts. This corpus contains 75,419 messages: 25220 ham and 50199 spam. The messages in this huge dataset are chronologically sorted and tagged using different anti spam filters.

Figure 13. Dredze Dataset: Sample Spam Images

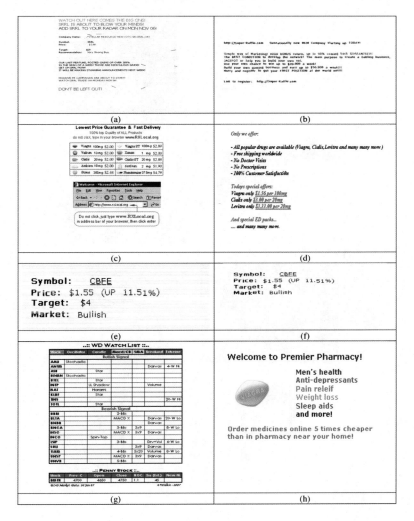

2.5.6. Other Datasets (CSMINING Group, 2010)

1. **Enron-Spam Datasets (Metsis, Androutsopoulos and Paliouras, 2006):**
    The datasets from the Enron corpus contain total 88792 messages. Out
    of these messages, 20170 spam messages and 16545 ham messages are
    in pre-processed format; while remaining 19089 spam messages and
    32988 ham messages are in their original/raw format.
2. **Ling-Spam Datasets (Androutsopoulos et al. 2000):** The datasets
    from the Linguist list consist of 2412 Linguist messages and 481 spam

Figure 14. Dredze Dataset: Sample Natural Images

messages. The legitimate messages are extracted from public achieves of mailing lists and more topic specific hence less standardized and conclusions based on this dataset can be limited.

3.   **PU1 Datasets (Androutsopoulos et al. 2000):** The PU1 datasets consist of 481 spam messages and 618 legitimate messages. It has been pre-processed by removing attachments and HTML tags. Fields other than "subject" are removed and each token (representing word, number, punctual symbols, etc.) are replaced by unique number to retain the privacy.

Table 1. Dredze dataset: Image formats

Sl no	Format	Ham	Spam
1	Bitmap	8	1
2	COM_File	15	30
3	EDU_File	4	--
4	EDU_SERV File	3	--
5	File	88	2
6	GIF File	563	3044
7	JPEG	1205	209
8	JPG	1	--
9	ORG	1	--
10	PNG	130	11
11	TIFF	3	--
12	Data Base File	--	1
13	DS_STORE File	--	1
Total		2021	3299

4. **Spam-Assassin Datasets (APACHE SPAMASSASSIN, 2003):** The datasets from Spam-Assassin public mail corpus consist of 1897 spam and 4150 legitimate messages.

5. **Spam Email Datasets (CSMINING Group, 2010):** The datasets consist of training set containing 2949 Ham messages and 1378 spam messages and the testing set containing 4292 messages without known class labels. It has become widely used standard in spam filter evaluation, due to its public and realistic nature.

2.6. IMAGE SPAM DATASET ANALYSIS

From these corpuses, one can say, image spam reflects following characteristics:

1. Generally, spam images are artificially generated.
2. As most of spam images are converted from text spam, their color components may be quite limited compared with natural scenes.
3. The spam images can belong to further different subcategories like spam with texts and artifacts or spam with icons etc. The spam images

Figure 15. SpamArchive Dataset: Sample Spam Images

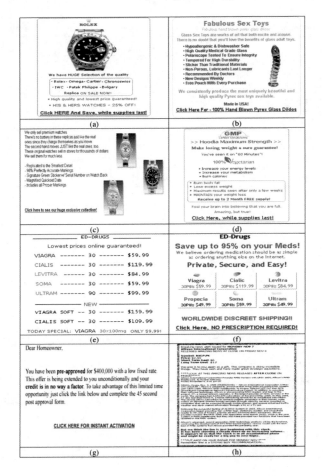

in the same class appear may very similar but quite different from other classes.

4. The image texture statistics of spam images are distinguishable from natural images.

5. Spammers tend to send the identical content many times to the same email account.

6. To evade from signature-based anti-spam detection techniques, spammers usually produce many variations for a template image spam using image operations like translation, rotation, scaling, local changes and adding random noises etc.

7. To convey information, most of image spam contains embedded text. A detailed analysis on both ham and spam corpus shows that, ham like natural images contain only pattern without any text or ham like photographed or scanned documents contain text; while image spam always contain some text with or without pattern in the background.

8. Color, luminosity and shape in natural images usually have a lot of noise, and such small, frequent changes can be detected as edges (Peng and Minoru, 2012). On the other hand, embedded text in an image tends to have even changes in the shape and color.

9. Although most of the legitimate e-mails will not have image attachments, it is problematic to consider all e-mails with image attachments as image spam (Umera and Tabata, 2008). In addition, there exist several image spam samples wherein the content being transmitted appears to be a legitimate e-mail because it contains words irrelevant to spam when text is included.

10. Most of the spam images are in the GIF or JPEG format as these formats compress an image in order to lower its file size. An image containing several alphabets has higher compressibility than a picture (Umera and Tabata, 2008).

11. Legitimate users do not transmit the same image to the same addressee several times. However, spammers transmit the same image several times in large quantities.

2.7. EXPERIMENTAL SETUP USED

Two corpora of spam e-mails were used for the experiments in this book: the publicly available Hunter Dataset (Gao et al. 2008) and Dredze Dataset (Dredze, Gevaryahu, and Elias, 2007). Intel core-i-5 3210M CPU- 2.5GHz and 2GB RAM is used with 64bit OS Windows-7. The experiments are carried out in MATLAB-2015 version.

2.8. CATEGORIZATION OF EXISTING IMAGE SPAM DETECTION TECHNIQUES

Existing image based spam techniques are categorized into two major domains - content based and non-content based filtering, as shown in Figure 16.

Figure 16. Image Spam Detection Techniques

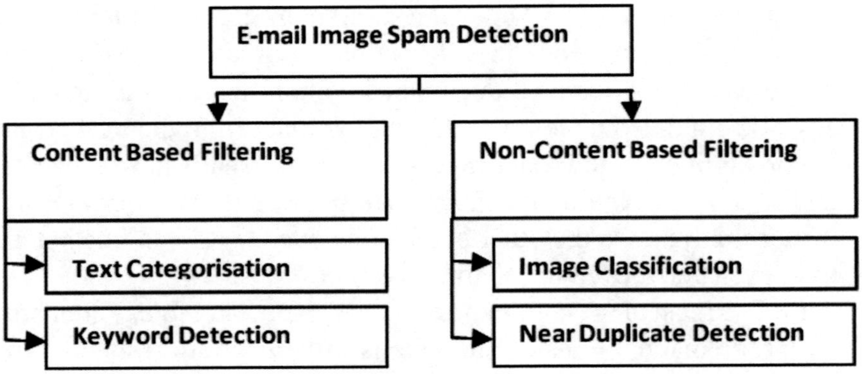

2.8.1. Content Based Filtering

Optical Character Recognition (OCR) technique extracts the embedded text character in the image and uses traditional text-based methods to filter the spam. The outputs of OCR are compared to some specific keywords or texts which are generally used in the spam emails. These techniques are further categorized into two sub categories.

Keyword Based Detection

A databank of keywords which are generally available in the spam emails is made and the output of the OCR is checked against these keywords. This technique has been used by Sanz in his work (Sanz, HidalgoGomez and Pérez, 2008). This approach is easy to implement and requires less processing time however requires frequent updation of databanks. OCR techniques are computationally demanding and can easily be fooled by image artefacts or obfuscating techniques (such as misspelling the keywords, scaling, rotation, translation, adding noise). High False positives are observed as presence of a single keyword can label the mail as spam. To overcome the OCR errors and to reduce false positives, Fuzzy OCR was introduced (Byun et al. 2007). This method takes into consideration the total number of keywords to define an image as spam, thus, higher the number of keywords found means higher the chance of an image to be spam.

Text Categorization

In these type of OCR based techniques, the text extracted from the non obfuscated images are used to label the mail as spam or ham. In present scenarios wherein the spammers use various obfuscation techniques, this technique may not yield reliable results.

2.8.2. Non-Content Based Filtering

Every image consists of variety of features which are exploited by the researchers to categorize an image as ham or spam. In these schemes these features are exploited for image spam detection. The various types of the image contents are file properties, High Level Characteristics (features) / metadata (such as height, width, format extension, file size and aspect ratio), global Low level image characteristics (features) like colour saturation, colour heterogeneity, text area in an image, shape, texture, etc. These features vary in both the classes of images so bifurcation of image based on these features against the test content can give more promising results. These are robust to various kinds of false artefacts introduced by the spammer. In these techniques, the image features are extracted from the collection of the ham and spam images. The collection of these features is called feature vector, which is used to train the classifier for classifying the images as spam or ham. The distinction between these techniques can be made on the basis of the feature vector and the type of classifier used (such as multiclass, two-class and one-class classifier). In multiple-class, images are categorised into several categories (such as transportation, commercial, banking, sexual, health, spiritual, sports, etc.). Two-class classifier is trained for two types of images whereas one-class classifiers trained either on spam or ham images. It is divided into two subparts.

Near-Duplicate Detection

Spam images are generated from the same templates (common base image) as they are sent to various recipients at the same time. Various spam images are generated by randomization of the objects or contents of these templates as a result a similarity is present among the spam images. This similarity property can be exploited by the classifier for discriminating them from ham. The classifier can be further trained on new data if the spam images are generated from different templates, which is not a frequent phenomenon as it is resources intensive.

Image Classification

In these techniques, dissimilarity between spam and ham image is decided based on the type of the high level and low level image feature selected for segregation. Most of the recent works use image features for spam detection, due to its robustness.

2.9. SUMMARY

This chapter has established rules to carry out a preliminary analysis to describe a spam mail. Further the chapter describes Image based spam, their characteristics and their generation methods in detail. The chapter brings out the limitations of existing spam detection techniques to handle image based spam. Finally it provides the details of the image spam dataset which are publicly available for the researchers and the detailed analysis of these spam databases. This chapter opens a path to visit the new research domain called image based spam detection, which has emerged recently due to the new challenges it has exposed to previous anti spam detection techniques.

REFERENCES

Androutsopoulos, I., Koutsias, J., Chandrinos, K. V., Paliouras, G., & Spyropoulos, C. D. (2000). An Evaluation of Naive Bayesian Anti-Spam Filtering. *Proceedings of the Workshop on Machine Learning in the New Information Age,11th European Conference on Machine Learning (ECML 2000)*, 9-17.

Androutsopoulos, I., Koutsias, J., Chandrinos, K. V., & Spyropoulos, C. D. (2000). An Experimental Comparison of Naive Bayesian and Keyword-Based Anti-Spam Filtering with Personal E-mail Messages. *Proceedings of the 23rd Annual International ACM SIGIR Conference on Research and Development in Information Retrieval*, 160-167. doi:10.1145/345508.345569

Apache Spam Assassin. (2003). *The Enterprise Open-Source Spam Filter*. Available from: http://spamassassin.apache.org/

Biggio, B., Fumera, G., Pillai, I., & Roli, F. (2007). Image Spam Filtering using Visual Information. *Proceedings of 14th International Conference on Image Analysis and Processing (ICIAP-2007)*, 105–110. doi:10.1109/ICIAP.2007.4362765

Byun, B., Lee, C. H., Webb, S., & Pu, C. (2007). A Discriminative Classifier Learning Approach to Image Modeling and Spam Image Identification. *Proceedings of 4th Conference on Email and Anti-Spam, (CEAS-2007)*.

CSMining Group. (2010). *Datasets*. Available from: http://www.csmining.org/index.php/data.html

Dredze, M., Gevaryahu, R., & Elias, B. A. (2007). Learning Fast Classifiers for Image Spam. *Proceedings of 4th International Conference on Email and Anti-Spam*.

Gao, Y., Yang, M., Zhao, X., Pardo, B., Wu, Y., Pappas, T. N., & Choudhary, A. N. (2008). Image Spam Hunter. *Proceedings of International Conference on Acoustics, Speech, and Signal Processing (ICASSP-2008)*, 1765–1768.

Giorgio, F., Pillai, I., & Fabio, R. (2006). Spam Filtering based on the Analysis of Text Information Embedded into Images. *Journal of Machine Learning Research*, 7, 2699–2720.

Gordan, C., & Tom, L. (2007). *SPAM Track Guidelines - TREC 2005 - 2007*. Available from: http://plg.uwaterloo.ca/~gvcormac/spam/

Harisinghaney, A., Dixit, A., Gupta, S., & Arora, A. (2014). Text and Image Based Spam Email Classifiation using KNN Naive Bayes and Reverse DBSCAN Algorithm. *Proceedings of International Conference on Reliability, Optimization and Information Technology (ICROIT-2014)*, 153-155.

Hazza, Z. M., & Aziz, N. A. (2012). Detecting Computer Generated Images for Image Spam Filtering. *Proceedings of 17th International Conference on Advanced Computer Science Applications and Technologies (ACSAT2012)*, 313-317. doi:10.1109/ACSAT.2012.38

He, P., Wen, X., & Zheng, W. (2009). A simple method for filtering image spam. *Proceedings of 8th IEEE/ACIS International Conference on Computer and Information Science (ICIS-2009)*, 910–913. doi:10.1109/ICIS.2009.101

Henry, C. (2008). *Luminance of Images*. Available from: http://www.cacs. louisiana.edu/~cice/lal/index.html

Hou, Y., Zhao, B., Zhang, H., & Yan, H. (2012). A fast image spam filter based on ORB. *Proceedings of 3rd IEEE International Conference on Network Infrastructure and Digital Content (IC-NIDC 2012)*, 503-507. doi:10.1109/ICNIDC.2012.6418804

Hsia, J., & Chen, M. (2009). Language-model-based Detection Cascade for Efficient Classification of Image-based Spam E-mail. *Proceedings of IEEE International Conference on Multimedia and Expo.(ICME-2009)*, 1182–1185.

Mehta, B., Nangia, S., Gupta, M., & Nejdl, W. (2008). Detecting Image Spam using Visual Features and Near Duplicate Detection. *Proceedings of 17th International Conference on World Wide Web. (www2008)*, 497–506. doi:10.1145/1367497.1367565

Metsis, V., Androutsopoulos, I., & Paliouras, G. (2006). Spam Filtering with Naive Bayes - Which Naive Bayes?. *Proceedings of the 3rd Conference on Email and Anti-Spam (CEAS-2006)*.

Peng, W., & Minoru, U. (2012). Spam Detection Using Sobel Operators and OCR. *Proceedings of 26th International Conference on Advanced Information Networking and Applications Workshops (WAINA-2012)*, 1017-1022.

Policypatrol. (2015). *How to Effectively Stop Spam and Junk Mail*. Available from: https://www.opswat.com/policypatrol/whitepapers/how-to-effectively-stop-spam-and-junk-mail/

Princeton. (2007). *Princeton Spam Image Benchmark*. Available from: http://www.cs.princeton.edu/cass/spam/

Qu, Z., & Zhang, Y. (2009). Filtering Image Spam using Image Semantics and Near-duplicate Detection. *Proceedings of 2nd International Conference on Intelligent Computation Technology and Automation (ICICTA-2009)*, 600–603. doi:10.1109/ICICTA.2009.151

Sanz, E. P., Hidalgomez, J. M., & Perezcortizo, J. C. (2008). *Email Spam Filtering. In Advances in Computers* (Vol. 74, pp. 45–114). Elsevier.

Uemura, M., & Tabata, T. (2008). Design and Evaluation of a Bayesian-filter-based Image Spam Filtering Method. *Proceedings of International Conference on Information Security and Assurance (ISA-2008)*, 46–51. doi:10.1109/ISA.2008.84

Wang, C., Zhang, F., Li, F., & Liu, Q. (2010). Image Spam Classification based on Low-level Image Features. *Proceedings of International conference on Communications, Circuits and Systems (ICCCAS-2010)*, 290-293.

Wang, Z., Josephson, W., Lv, Q., Charikar, M., & Li, K. (2007). Filtering Image Spam with Near-duplicate Detection. *Proceedings of 4th International Conference on Email and Anti-spam (CEAS-2007)*.

Ward, V. W., & Aiko, P. (2010). Filtering Spam from Bad Neighbourhoods. *International Journal of Network Management, Wiley, 20*(6), 433–444. doi:10.1002/nem.753

Zhang, C., Chen, W., Chen, X., Tiwari, R., Yang, L., & Warner, G. (2009). A Multimodal Data Mining Framework for Revealing Common Sources of Spam Images. *Journal of Multimedia, 4*(5), 313–320. doi:10.4304/jmm.4.5.313-320

Zuo, H., Hu, W., Wu, O., Chen, Y., & Luo, G. (2009). Detecting Image Spam Using Local Invariant Features and Pyramid Match Kernel. *Proceedings of 18th International conference on World Wide Web (WWW 2009)*, 1187–1188. doi:10.1145/1526709.1526921

Zuo, H., Li, X., Wu, O., Hu, W., & Luo, G. (2009). Image Spam Filtering using Fourier-mellin Invariant Features. *Proceedings of International Conference on Acoustics, Speech, and Signal Processing (ICASSP-2009)*, 849–852.

Chapter 3

Image Spam:
Feature Extraction

ABSTRACT

Spam features represent the unique and special characteristics associated with spam, which are further used to differentiate them from other genuine messages. Each message m is processed by a feature extraction module to represent m in terms of n dimensional feature vector $x = (x_1, x_2, ..., x_n)$ containing n features. This feature vector consists of many such features extracted from spam. In case of text based spam filters, a feature can be a word and a feature vector may be composed of various words extracted from spam. Each spam is associated with one feature vector. Based on the characteristics discussed in previous chapter, we will try to extract different features capturing those unique characteristics from image spam, in order to build the robust spam detection algorithms further. These features are broadly classified into high level metadata features, low level image features like color features, grayscale features, texture related features and embedded text related features.

3.1. HIGH-LEVEL METADATA FEATURES

High-level Meta data features such as image width, height, aspect ratio, file size, compression and image area can be extracted from the image header for spam image categorization (He, Wen and Zheng, 2009, Wang et al., 2010). Figure 1, Figure 2, Figure 3 and Figure 4 shows the distribution of features related to File Size (say, Feature *Image_FileSize*), Image Area (say, Feature

DOI: 10.4018/978-1-68318-013-5.ch003

Image Spam

Figure 1. Histogram of file size of spam and natural images

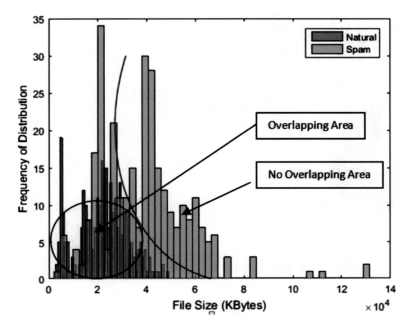

Figure 2. Histogram of image area of spam and natural images

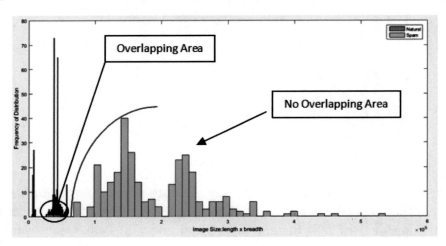

Figure 3. Histogram of compression ratio of spam and natural images

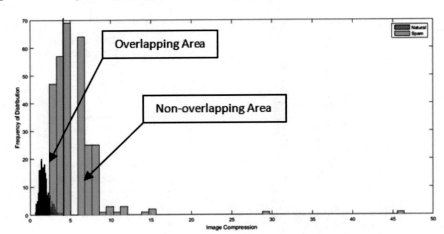

Figure 4. Histogram of aspect ratio of spam and natural images

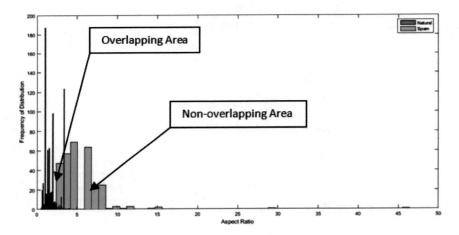

Image_Area), Compression Ratio (say, Feature *Compression_Ratio*) and Aspect Ratio (say, Feature *Aspect_Ratio*) respectively for the hunter dataset containing total of 600 images (300 spam and 300 ham means genuine images). These metadata features are easy to analyse and needs less processing time so these are extracted from both ham and spam images, can be useful to distinguish Natural Images and Spam Images. If $I = \{i(i,j), 0 \leq i \leq m, 0 \leq j \leq n\}$ represents two dimensional image with *length* = *m* and *width* = *n* then *Image_Area, Compression_Ratio* and *Aspect_Ratio* are given as in Equation 3.1, Equation 3.2 and Equation 3.3 respectively.

$$Image \_ Area = m \times n \tag{3.1}$$

$$Compression \_ Ratio = \frac{Image \_ Area}{File \_ Size} \tag{3.2}$$

$$Aspect \_ Ratio = \frac{m}{n} \tag{3.3}$$

3.1.1. File Size

Spam images are generally has more file size as compared to ham images. Figure 1 shows the histogram of the file size for the above said dataset. As it is clear from the figure that the file size of spam images vary from 0 to 13×10^4 Kbytes whereas it vary from 0 to 5×10^4 Kbytes. So it can be a very good feature to segregate the spam images in first layer of any hierarchical model (Feng et al., 2011). So threshold of file size should be choose in such a way that it gives very less false positive and false negative in any algorithm. As it is clear from the figure, that if threshold lies in the overlapping area than the error will be introduced in the result.

3.1.2. Image Area

Many spam images are generally banners, due to which they have different dimensions of length and breadth. Figure 2 shows the histogram of the area for the above said dataset. It is clear from the Figure 2, that the file size of spam images vary from 0.3 to 5.5×10^5; whereas it vary from 0 to 0.7×10 for ham images. The distribution shows little overlapping between spam and genuine images; hence this feature can be exploited in the first layer of spam detection hierarchical model. The area size value should be choose in such a way that it gives very less false positive and false negative in any algorithm. As it is clear from the figure that if threshold lies in the overlapping area than the error will be introduced in the result whereas if it is in non-overlapping area the results will be more accurate.

3.1.3. Compression Ratio

Ham images are generally less compressed as compared to the ham images. This can be easily understood in Figure 3 which depicts the histogram of the compression ratio for the above said dataset. It is because the spammers want to send the spam in such a manner that the message can be given to the end user with less expenditure cost of sending the mail, more the size of the image more will be the cost for using the more bandwidth. As it is clear from the figure that the compression ratio of spam images varies from 0 to 46% whereas it varies from 0 to 4% for ham images. This feature can be exploited for detecting the spam images in any multilayer model. If it is used along with some other low level features, it will provide more accuracy.

3.1.4. Aspect Ratio

This feature have the same characteristic to that of the compression ratio as ham images are generally have less aspect ratio as compared to the ham images. This can be easily understood in Figure 4 which depicts the histogram of the compression ratio for the above said dataset. In order to incur less expenditure in sending the spam to the user the spammers want the spam images of lesser aspect ratio. As it is clear from the figure that the aspect ratio of spam images varies from 0 to 4% whereas it varies from 0 to 46% for ham images. However the aspect ratio of spam images are generally from 4 to 46% as it is easily analyzed in Figure 4. So similar to other metadata features this feature information should always be taken into consideration for detecting the spam images in any multilayer model. It can also be combined with other low level features to improve the results.

Extraction of high level meta-data features is simpler and involves less computational cost. These meta data features can be extracted without fully decoding the images, hence offers fast spam detection (He, Wen and Zheng, 2009, Feng et al., 2011). The total processing time required to extract these features from 300 Natural Images and 300 Spam Images was 2.73 seconds on Intel Core i-5 machine with 2GB RAM and Matlab R2015a version.

Krasser (2007) exploited high level features including width, height, format and file size are exploited for spam detection. The model was based on C4.5

tree algorithm with SVM classifier and supported fast detection. However, the model was capable of eliminating only 60% of the image spam with false positive rate = 0.5%. The author suggested utilization of proposed model as the first layer in any multilayer hierarchical spam detection model; where, other layers can utilize expensive low level features for refining the results (Krasser et al., 2007). He, Wen and Zheng (2009) utilized meta data feature based filtering in the first stage of spam detector followed by histogram filtering for suspected spam images in the second stage. In case of small sized large resolution GIF images, meta data feature based model may not be effective. The features like file size of spam images may become very similar to those ham GIF images.

Uemura and Tabata (2008) proposed a spam detection based on meta-data features extracted from GIF images (which accounts for majority of image spam) with Bayesian filter. The experimental results indicates that the proposed technique can realize a false negative rate lower than that of the conventional Bayesian filter technique.

Using only high level image features does not guarantee good accuracy. Hence, to increase the spam detection accuracy, these features are generally combined with other low-level image features. Peizhou et al. (2008) utilized low level Image features like Image Size, Width, Height, Bit Depth, and Aspect Ratio, along with high level gray histogram and color histogram features.

3.2. COLOR FEATURES

Utilizing color features instead of gray level features, may increase the detection accuracy; as color features contains more information than that of gray level features (He, Wen and Zheng, 2009). Figure 5 (a) and 5 (b) shows sample natural image and its color histogram respectively; while Figure 5 (c) and 5 (d) shows sample spam image and its color histogram respectively. In general, image spam show evidence of many important properties (Policypatrol, 2016) including color attributes, which would raise the suspicion in the minds of anti spam analysts.

Zhang et al. (2009), replaced each pixel in a color image into a 6-bit color-code by taking the 2 most significant bits of each R, G, and B color components. This process replaces similar colors within a range by a single value, and makes easy to compare color histograms by analyzing histogram of color-codes only. Figure 6 (a) and 6 (b) shows the histogram of color-codes for sample natural and spam images respectively.

Figure 5. Color histogram for sample natural and spam image

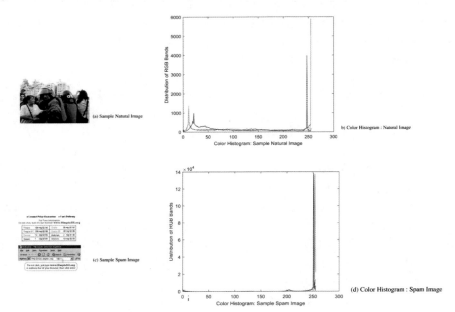

3.2.1. Color Saturation Features

Color saturation is quantified as the fraction of the total number of pixels in the image for which the difference $\max(R, G, B) - \min(R, G, B)$ is greater than some threshold T (Wang et al., 2010). We evaluate this fraction for both text and non-text parts of the image separately, leading to two color saturation features. When compared with images of natural scenes, we expect the spam images to be generally more saturated due to the presence of synthetic graphics. However, when compared with generic computer-generated graphics images, we expect the spam images to be less saturated due to the presence of natural elements.

3.2.2. Color Heterogeneity Features

First, the original color image is scaled by the maximum possible intensity such that the intensities in the RGB channels are within the range [0, 1]; it is then converted to an indexed image using minimum variance quantization such that the number of colors in the indexed image is at most k (Byun et al., 2007). The RMS errors between the original image and the indexed image

Figure 6. Color-code histogram for sample natural and spam image

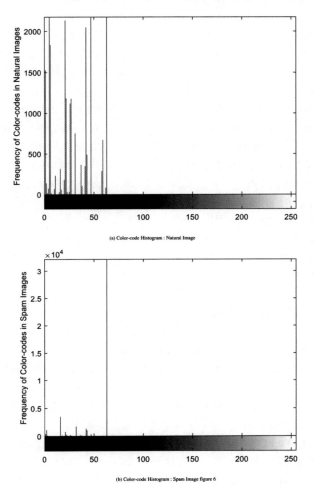

(a) Color-code Histogram : Natural Image

(b) Color-code Histogram : Spam Image figure 6

are then calculated individually for the text and non-text parts of the image, which form two color heterogeneity features. We choose $k=10$ for non-text portions and $k=8$ for text portions. Since the graphical portions of spam images comprise far fewer colors than natural scene images, we expect their heterogeneity to be lower.

Various characteristics of color in various color spaces are utilized by the researcher's in order to make a robust anti-spam image detection technique. Histogram of any feature captured from both spam and genuine dataset represents distribution of data and hence summarize a set of data effectively. Parametric statistics like mean and standard deviation are used as simple summaries of a set of data, when the data are roughly Gaussian. Similarly other statistics like discreteness, variance, kurtosis and skewness can be considered along with mean and standard deviation. Here, mean refers to the average (expected value) of all elements of histogram/set of values. Variance is a non-negative value which represents how far the data points are deviated from the mean. Small value of variance indicates that the data points tend to be very close to the mean (expected value); while a high variance indicates that the data points are very spread out around the mean and from each other. Skewness measures symmetry of distribution. Entropy of histogram measures histogram dispersion. It also specifies the uncertainty in the image values. Low Entropy means that the distribution varies, it has peaks and valleys. Kurtosisa measures whether the data are heavy-tailed or light-tailed relative to a normal distribution. For each feature, we can calculate these statistical values and their distribution can be plotted.

3.2.3. RGB Color Space

1. Red Channel Properties Experiments are carried out to calculate different statistical properties for the red component or red channel (see Figure 7) and it has been noticed that discreteness, mean, skewness and entropy gives the clear demarcating border for detecting spam from ham images. These features along with the metadata feature will always give the promising results.
2. Green Channel Properties: Experiments are carried out to calculate the statistical properties for the green component or channel (see Figure 8) and it has been noticed that discreteness, mean, skewness and entropy gives the clear demarcating border for detecting spam from ham images. These features along with the metadata feature will always give the promising results.
3. Blue Channel Properties: Experiments are carried out to calculate the above said properties for the blue component or blue channel and (see Figure 9) it has been noticed that discreteness, mean, skewness and entropy gives the clear demarcating border for detecting spam from ham images. These features along with the metadata feature will always give the promising results.

Figure 7. Histogram of Red Channel Characteristics

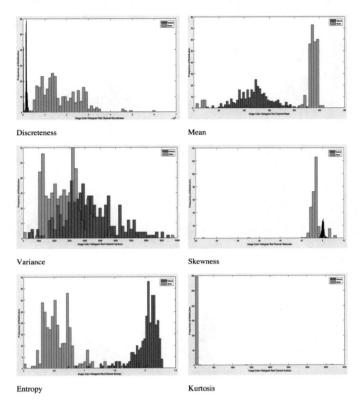

Discreteness   Mean

Variance   Skewness

Entropy   Kurtosis

All the three color shows the same characteristics and produces the similar results so any of these colors can be utilized as the low level feature in RGB color space to segregate the spam images from that of ham images.

Soranamageswari and Meena (2010) combined RGB histogram properties with HSV (Hue, Saturation and Value based model) histogram properties to get good image spam detection rate. Here, hue of a color refers to which pure color it resembles means that all shades of red will have the same hue. Saturation of a color describes how white the color is means a pure red will have saturation of 1 while shades of red will have saturations less than 1. White will have a saturation of 0. The value of a color describes darkness of the color with black color reflecting value of 0 and the value increases as the color moves away from black. Figure 10 (a)-(f) shows the distribution of mean and variances for all these three components in case of both spam and ham images.

Figure 8. Histogram of Green Channel Characteristics

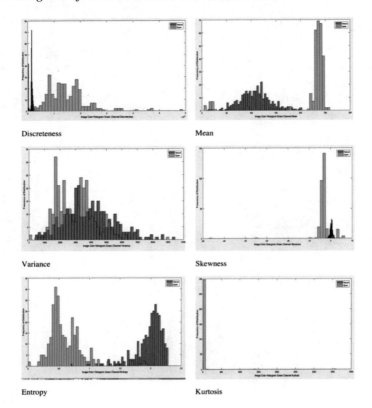

3.3. GRAYSCALE VALUE FEATURES

Experiments are carried out to calculate the above said properties for the grayscale component / channel (see Figure 11) and it has been noticed that discreteness, mean, skewness and entropy gives the clear demarcating border for detecting spam from ham images. These features along with the metadata feature will always give the promising results.

3.4. TEXTURE RELATED FEATURES

Following are few important texture related features extracted from both ham and spam images, which may be useful to distinguish them. To extract image texture features, we can use image processing and computer vision tools available such as Matlab image processing toolbox, OpenCV, MaZda, etc.

Figure 9. Histogram of Blue Channel Characteristics

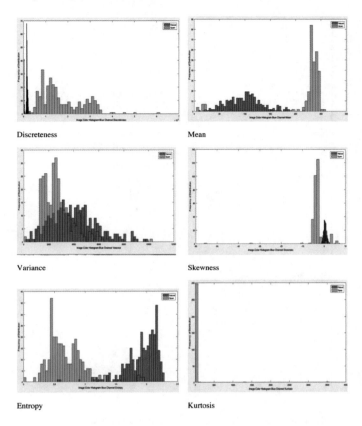

Discreteness   Mean

Variance   Skewness

Entropy   Kurtosis

3.4.1. Image Texture with DWT

Various researchers have used texture feature of the image to demarcate the spam from the ham images as generally spam are computer generated due to which they have a different texture patter as compared to that of natural / ham images. DWT is one of the transforms to capture the texture information (Basheer, 2011); however it can be seen in the Figure 12, that it has the overlapping are due to which there will be more false positives and the overall accuracy will be less.

Figure 10. HSV histogram characteristics

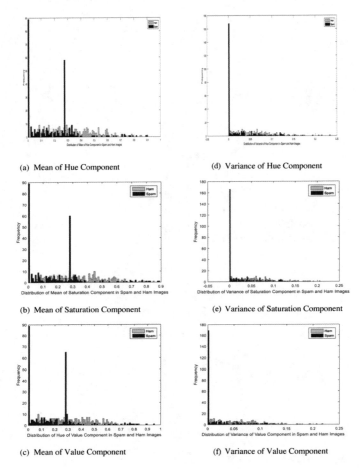

(a) Mean of Hue Component

(d) Variance of Hue Component

(b) Mean of Saturation Component

(e) Variance of Saturation Component

(c) Mean of Value Component

(f) Variance of Value Component

3.4.2. Run-Length Matrix (RLM)

The run-length matrix p(i,j) is the number of runs with pixels of gray level i and run length j (Basheer, 2011). Various texture features like Short Run Emphasis (SRE), Gray Level Non-Uniformity (GLN), Run Percentage (RP), Run Length Non-Uniformity (RLN), Low Gray Level Run Emphasis (LGRE), High Gray Level Run Emphasis (HGRE) can be derived from RLM. To derive RLM features, images are converted to grayscale and quantized using 16 quantization levels. The RLM features are computed for vertical, horizontal, 45 and 135 degree directions. Figure 13 (a)-(f) shows the distribution of RLM features in both spam and ham images respectively. Out of these features, RP and LGRE shows less overlapping compared to all other features.

Figure 11. Histogram of gray scale values characteristics

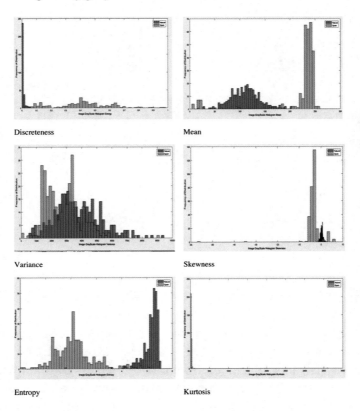

Figure 12. Histogram of Texture by DWT

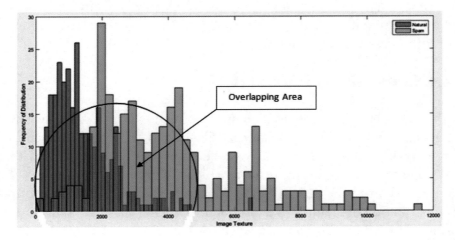

Figure 13. RLM Features

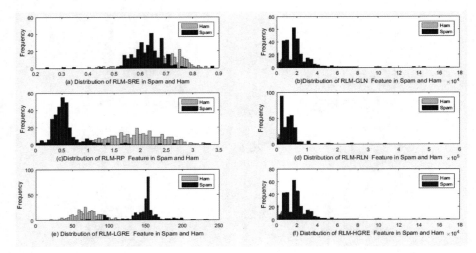

3.4.3. Gray Level Co-Occurrence Matrix (GLCM)

GLCM is a matrix that is defined over an image to be the distribution of co-occurring values at a given offset (Basheer, 2011). GLCM characterize the texture of an image by calculating how often pairs of pixel with specific values and in a specified spatial relationship occur in an image. From this matrix, different statistical measures like contrast, correlation, energy and homogeneity can be extracted for further analysis (Francesco and Carlo, 2008). Figure 14 (a)-(d) shows the distribution of contrast, correlation, energy and homogeneity statistical texture measures calculated from GLCM matrix of both spam and ham images. Here, GLCM energy feature shows wider separation in spam and ham images.

3.4.4. Local Binary Pattern (LBP)

LBP operator is applied to encode texture information of both spam and natural images efficiently (Gao, Choudhary and Gang, 2010). LBP operator labels the image pixels by thresholding the 3 x 3 neighborhood of each pixel with the center value and considers the result as a binary number. The properties of the histogram of these $2^8 = 256$ different labels are used as a texture descriptor. The distribution of features like discreteness, mean, variance, skewness and kurtosis of LBP histogram is analyzed for both spam and natural grayscale images as shown in Figure 15.

Figure 14. GLCM Features

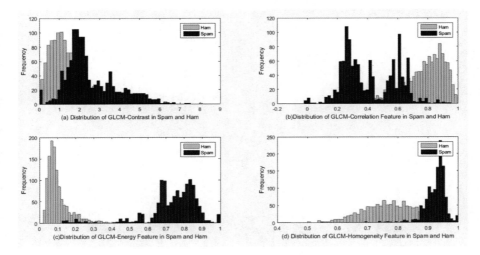

Experiments are carried out to calculate the LBP histogram of above said properties for capturing the texture and it has been noticed that discreteness, mean, and variance gives the clear demarcating border for detecting spam from ham images. These features along with the metadata feature will always give the promising results.

3.4.5. Image Gradient Features

Image gradient represents directional change in the intensity/color in an image and is capable of capturing textural properties of an image (Soranamageswari and Meena, 2011). Figure 15 (a)-(f) shows that the distribution of discreteness, mean, and variance of image gradient feature gives the clear demarcating border for detecting spam from ham images. These features along with the metadata feature will always give the promising results. The authors in their work used these features as key features for spam detection (Soranamageswari and Meena, 2011). These features are normalized before giving to feed forward back propagation neural network (BPNN) model in order to achieve the average classification accuracy of around 93.7% on 9/10 training and testing sets in (Soranamageswari and Meena, 2011).

Figure 15. LBP histogram of various characteristics to capture texture

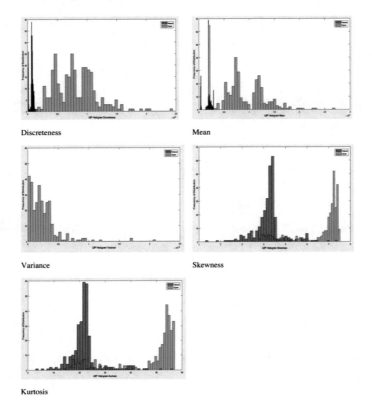

Discreteness   Mean

Variance   Skewness

Kurtosis

3.4. SHAPE RELATED FEATURES

In order to capture the shape related features, following parameters were utilized and their distribution in both ham and spam dataset is given in Figure 17 (a)-(e) respectively.

1. Number of Edges using Canny edge detector (Gao, Choudhary and Gang, 2010)
2. – (g) Oriented Gradient Histograms of means, variance, skewness,, entropy, Kurtosis and Discreetness are calculated
3. Anisotropy of Energy
4. Energy Difference between LF and HF DWT subband (Gao, Choudhary and Gang, 2010)
5. Average Length of Edges using Canny edge detector (Gao, Choudhary and Gang, 2010)

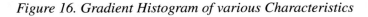

Figure 16. Gradient Histogram of various Characteristics

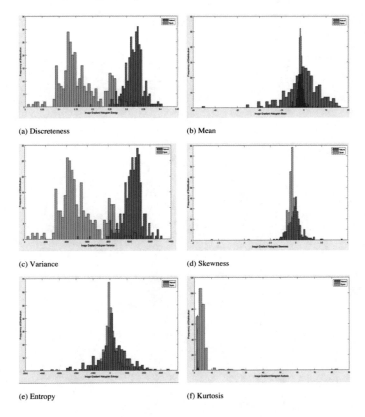

(a) Discreteness   (b) Mean

(c) Variance   (d) Skewness

(e) Entropy   (f) Kurtosis

It has been noticed that the entropy, mean, Energy Difference in LF and HF sub-band (Gao, Choudhary and Gang, 2010), and Discreetness of Oriented Gradients gives the most promising results. So these features can always be exploited independently or in combination with other high level features for designing the detection model.

The authors of research work (Peng and Uehara, 2012) proposed a new feature called ratio of edge curve to area which captures spam image property that it generally contains text. Both standard Sobel operator and diagonal Sobel operator are used to calculate the ratio of edge curve to area to detect image spam. Figure 18 (a)-(c) show the distribution of ratio of edge curve to area using horizontal, vertical and diagonal Sobel operators. Woods, Longe, and Roberts (2012) also used Sobel filter to extract the edge features for image spam detection. They calculated the percentage of the total number of pixels in the whole image which are edges and found that the value of this

Figure 17. Shape related features

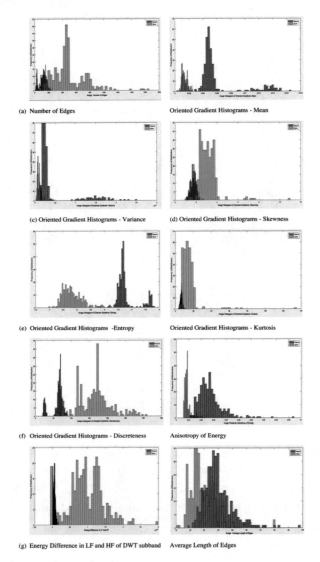

(a) Number of Edges   Oriented Gradient Histograms - Mean

(c) Oriented Gradient Histograms - Variance   (d) Oriented Gradient Histograms - Skewness

(e) Oriented Gradient Histograms -Entropy   Oriented Gradient Histograms - Kurtosis

(f) Oriented Gradient Histograms - Discreteness   Anisotropy of Energy

(g) Energy Difference in LF and HF of DWT subband   Average Length of Edges

percentage is more in case of computer generated spam images compared to that of the natural images.

The distribution of this proposed single feature in spam and ham images shows a lot of overlapping in selected features hence detection accuracy may get affected largely. In case, spam with pattern and ham with character is difficult to differentiate because of the differences in the number of characters

Figure 18. Distribution of ratio of edge curve to area

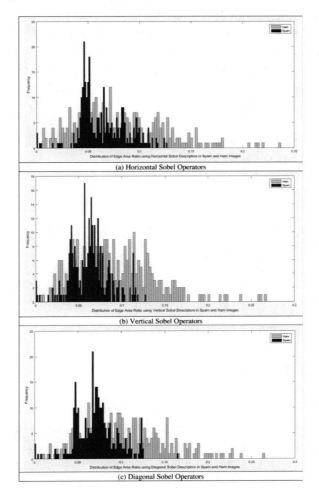

in images. The suggested method is also vulnerable to additive noise generally added in the spam images.

3.5. EMBEDDED TEXT RELATED FEATURES

Spam images contain embedded text carrying advertisements. The features extracted from the embedded text will help to describe the content. Embedded-text within images can be natural scene text - that appears as part of the scene in images and artificial text - is manually added. Algorithm to extract the embedded features is as stated in Algorithm 1. In the pre-processing step, after converting the image into binary image, flood fill operation carried out to remove irrelevant artefacts from images. Then the number of connected objects in the binary image is calculated to know how many number of letter present in the text. The region properties of the image for each connected component object in the binary image are calculated to get the area of the entire letter.

```
Algorithm 1. To Extract Text Area and Word Boxes
Algorithm_to_extract_TextArea_and_WordBoxes
1. Read Image(x)
2. b = Convert_to_Binary Image(x)
2. i = Invert_Binary Image(b)
3. Fill_Holes_in_Binary Image(i)
4. Label_Connected_Components_in_BinaryImage(i)
5. Calculate_RegionProperties_BinaryImage(i)
6. Form_BoundingBox_BinaryImage(i)
7. Number of WordBoxes = Get_NumberofWordBoxes(i)
8. n_t = Get_TotalNumberofPixelsContributintoTextRegion(i)
```

$$9. \quad TextArea = \frac{n_t}{length(x) \times breadth(x)} \times 100\%$$

3.5.1. Image Text Area

It refers to the pixel count ratio of the detected text regions to that of the overall image area. As it can be seen that very less overlapping area is present in this feature due to which good accuracy can be achieved. Figure 18 shows the distribution of image text area feature extracted from both spam and ham image dataset respectively.

3.5.2. Image Word Boxes

Image word boxes refer to the total number of text regions detected in spam images.This feature has more overlapping area due to which it is inferior to image text area feature (see Figure 19).

Congfu, Yafang and Kevin, (2010) proposed a novel approach based on Base64 encoding of image files and n-gram technique for feature extraction. The images are transformed into Base64 presentation as shown in Figure 20 (a)-(b). The extracted n-gram features were used to train an SVM. The authors claimed good detection accuracy as well as its practicability due

Figure 19. Distribution of Text Area in Spam and Ham Images

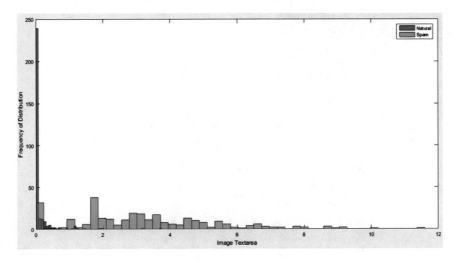

Figure 20. Distribution of Image word Boxes in Spam and Ham Images

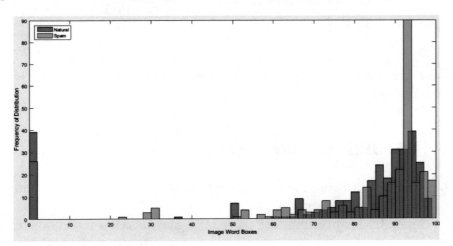

Figure 21. Sample Ham Image and its Base64 Representation

SEpXPyZTCBQfCQYCPzgDHgsLEB0HFBdMT1gwZYO6//J9/Pz8+f72QOLh5LBmilNplxYeYdGeYn3F
S4Njd5KUk2WQmEaFeJ5tkX52fmx/ZGc+RTAcSX+SlJh3jcbFpMSusa+krbGrsrKjuH+LkmJ+z45z
lG95ZlBIhluKiKh8iZxxlrCkiKK1km52jrayo7CsjohxfrWwlJiMlHWwdI2ymJCwra2uvJiYsa2r
mmd5d4Splrm1K4JeKycyFhQWHSgYQ4UmslEEJRYNAX6ISWl/Kyzk/P78/fz+/fT9/c54mZVtoXhZ
NSlDXTdHWDqEX5F0gJyBnJqPd0hfgoeCiJ1dYJheRhgbb0gzHnCck5KMjcu+scC9pr2joayyta2d
taZtmYKA0pl7hnJ4bXNiI2WVf4FrpYCBmaammbG/hHGQr6uKrL23inNsdqWrtoyHloWArranm5iw
mbq5tqmbtMeebm1raoeZlKimOCk6NEwVGxsOBhkqTJVHzVcHFwkRAVhDTtpZSk/V/f37/v78/f77
+v7RvIV2i59XRxcaGB6nYUBzs5Sbi5OVdolIKmlzh2BgipujbnJHV1MnV4RnamSEm4yShbPDvcS9
qsCYn6WvtqCho7KXinyZs5dze39taGxvi4Nxk4mFrYuRpaiSl8x7loqBnq+XsqW2hXVwhqO7hoK0
lo+IssmYkaOjraKmvMaZuM+NZHqBdoWPlpyhihUHOHwyDh8SBgFfmT5KvyJuOQ8eXBo6feymbpCh
/Pn+/vf+/v3+/Pz8+JNwZYJ+LC0UISwpR0g1PKN5cJecj4CfSWhhemdomZSob05LQURZYG1mgYFn
oZmVgbXOu7q9uMKmvaGhvJ2Zsa2QjHKQtpJwhX5banInjYmHmHpjqoOXn5iVm71opYZ8sK6Hr7Ck
flqKdqumq4fAmoaOxaicjpKoqbeyysGfmsmpXoBiaoKRk5WdZ0cuC66/KglVEgstVGOZKl5IKhQd
WnUwZ7TOuoGl/clFsf3+/fr+/v3597ZsZFB8NTcXRT8kUEspS4iSjX5+h3eHmUhdfXyBpltvj2E6
W1QqT1WUblSAe32Wgbi6xcHBuL2IvKChun6PyK18n2WGpKlrh4JsZ3VjooCnd3N1snCcnK6PqrF2
kayRpZqeqq+yp5CCeeh9op2L4p2zyaCfqpWqs6DG2b/FncG8h3h3Jmcohlp2od2oUWYmOqokCaqAD
QZkm6/1WEzsXBhYsjNjfeDoj/a04Iv36///9+ejRdVNsakFOViUaMUEwUEgtP4aPkJSck5Klf0pp
pXxfoKKFkG0/TUk4anSGf2GYjHqNga24v8O0qMa2sSmu3qkfK6TgHiDn6NxlYJ7anhtr4eUdXaD
omypiZ6nr46CsLyWpai7oqS3vJxjj9C0mpyn9ZGyz6WflS2zvardwNiqrbuwfZp5b3SlmZypxoUn
OUNKeGhcilWK/LlZ2XU4HiYCDx1VREubfCxvYas/hv3//vv93Of70lxITFBAWDE4Ris0VURARkqZ
p5uPilSKcF9gfn9+mXWJJ3BmUGdJZISRe1uVjpB7d6zQssG/qMGvnqaetoafapq5gXB8klqI4uA
Z3R6a6itdYh/kXDDZJ27paaCIMKDpLCdn7espp1fn7Grr5eqx4qvzqaMm7OosLzAx9nFvsSunSp5
bGqamomOfG1NKItIKENTOSPB0ClOSYAednsCEQoyLxJGbVqRhpkjdvj5/fn8tH6XU1x4XV59dJm0
wYogUkdIXUt1nJ6qn46MeZabWI6Bql9+nl5yS4mDZWG0hHaXmliPg6a6tL6zt7yxoqeLtamTg5iq
iWaEm7dpJob1cHblpo6Xdmxwomi8g7+molaLlmqSLolyfyK+7qp1toRW6mrKigoews7WTolJGwrmy

to less running time compared to other high level textual or visual feature based methods.

3.6. FEATURE SET ANALYSIS

From these corpuses, one can say, image spam reflects following characteristics:

1. Generally, spam images are artificially generated low resolution images with many random noises. Thus, compared to natural images, they have poorer quality and lack visual details.
2. As most of spam images are converted from text spam, their color components may be quite limited compared with natural scenes.
3. Most of the spam images are not natural scenes images but artificial images synthesized on computer. Hence, they do not have continuous texture features as natural images. Hence, we can say, the image texture statistics of spam images are distinguishable from natural images.

4. Large portions of spam images contain only text messages, which is seldom to see in case of natural images.

5. Due to the limitation of transmission time and bandwidth, spam images are usually relatively small with limited image height, width, area, and other image attributes.

6. A higher compression ratio format is often used in spam images.

7. The spam images can belong to further different subcategories like spam with texts and artefacts or spam with icons etc. The spam images in the same class appear may very similar but quite different from other classes.

8. Spammers tend to send the identical content many times to the same email account.

9. To evade from signature-based anti-spam detection techniques, spammers usually produce many variations for a template image spam using image operations like translation, rotation, scaling, local changes and adding random noises etc.

10. To convey information, most of image spam contains embedded text. A detailed analysis on both ham and spam corpus shows that, ham like natural images contain only pattern without any text or ham like photographed or scanned documents contain text; while image spam always contain some text with or without pattern in the background.

11. Color, luminosity and shape in natural images usually have a lot of noise, and such small, frequent changes can be detected as edges. On the other hand, embedded text in an image tends to have even changes in the shape and color.

12. Although most of the legitimate e-mails will not have image attachments, it is problematic to consider all e-mails with image attachments as image spam. In addition, there exist several image spam samples wherein the content being transmitted appears to be a legitimate e-mail because it contains words irrelevant to spam when text is included.

13. Most of the spam images are in the GIF or JPEG format as these formats compress an image in order to lower its file size. An image containing several alphabets has higher compressibility than a picture.

14. Legitimate users do not transmit the same image to the same addressee several times. However, spammers transmit the same image several times in large quantities.

15. In order to maintain good readability, spam images use sufficient foreground or background contrast.

16. Generally, background area of image spam is composed of one or more dominant colors. It also occupies significant portions of an image and exhibits more uniformity, compared to foreground illustrations. (Zhang et al., 2009)

3.7. FEATURE SELECTION AND DIMENSION REDUCTION

Different extracted features have different dynamic ranges; hence once an n-dimensional feature vector $x(i) \equiv (x_1, x_2, ..., x_n)$ is extracted from given image dataset containing $x(i), 0 \leq i \leq m$ images, normalization is applied to the columns in order to limit all the values of a certain feature in a specific range. Before feature analysis and selection, the features are first scaled. This also prevents overweighing some features over others. For normalization, each column is scanned for the maximum value and then all the values in that particular column will be divided by this maximum value. If $\left[f_{\min}, f_{\max} \right]$ denotes dynamic range of a feature f in given image then scaled/normalized feature $\bar{f}$ is given as in Equation (3.4).

$$\bar{f} = \frac{f - f_{\min}}{f_{\max} - f_{\min}} \tag{3.4}$$

Based on distributions of various features, that we have stated here; it may not be appropriate to consider only one of the features. Single set of feature may not be true representative of actual samples for e.g. if one chooses only File_Size feature for classification and says that image spam files are lower in size compared to that of ham. Then no matter how we choose the threshold for file size; we cannot reliably separate spam from ham by considering file size alone. Hence, it is important to consider multiple more discriminating features for good classification.

Further, considering features from multiple domains increases the size of feature space. All extracted features may not reflect good separability. Selecting separable features also enhances the accuracy of model. We can use feature scoring techniques like Fisher criterion to select features reflecting good separability. In feature selection techniques, a subset of best terms is selected and ranked out of the original set of terms. Further, many features carry the same information and there is a correlation between features. Hence all selected huge feature space does not necessarily provide good results. In order to improve the efficiency of spam classifier, dimensionality reduction step is required, in which a number of elements used to represent a message will be reduced using feature selection technique. We can use Principal Components Analysis (PCA) feature selection algorithm resulting into a new feature space with only few major components. These components are combination of the most important features from the original feature space. Recent research shows that many low-level image features could be helpful in distinguishing spam (Liu et al., 2010). However, the representation power of these low-level image features is explicitly examined in terms of how and to what extent each subset of the individual features can be used to distinguish between spam and ham images. This helps to identify beneficial features from redundant ones improves classifier's performance. The authors proposed an effective stepwise regression algorithm based on the Minimum Description Length (MDL) Principle. (Liu et al., 2010) to perform sparse model selection in such a high dimensional feature space.

Using only low level features is time and processor expensive while using only high level features is less computational intensive but does not guarantee good detection accuracy. Hence, both high level and low level features are extracted from various domains in order to increase the accuracy of the detection system (Dredze, Gevaryahu and Bachrach, 2007). The authors used both metadata and visual features using one-class SVM classifier with radial basis function (RBF) kernel (Wang et al., 2010). The authors stated a detection rate of 95% for various datasets. Feng et al. (2011) proposed Multi-modal feature extraction from both text and image of email to build multiple classifiers. The fusion method is used in order to choose the output of multiple classifiers with P-SVM method.

Further, so far we have tacitly assumed that the consequences of our decision making actions are equally costly i.e. deciding ham as spam when in fact it is a ham is just as cost undesirable as the converse. Such symmetry in the cost may not be useful as, general users may not like their ham mails to be marked as spam. While they may easily accept occasional image spam marked as ham. Hence, it is useful to adjust or move our decision boundary to avoid any ham to be marked as spam. There is an overall single cost associated with our decision, and we need to set a decision boundary so as to minimize this cost.

3.8. CLASSIFIERS

Generally, a given image datatset is divided into a train and test sets. Two different class labels 'Spam' and 'Ham' are used to categorize the image in dataset as spam image and a legitimate image respectively. Different machine learning classifiers like C4.5 Decision Tree (DT), Support Vector Machine (SVM), Multilayer Perception (MP), Naive Bayes (NB), Bayesian Network (BN), and Random Forest (RF) can be used for classification. The classifier/ model is generally trained on training dataset, usually chosen large size to make the model more generalized and achieve good accuracy. The trained model is validated against test dataset. Weka tool can be used for applying these machine learning techniques. Weka accepts the features expressed in .arff (attribute relation file format) or .csv format (Lamia, Munesh and Mohammadi, 2012).

The classifier algorithm should offer fast detection as well as high detection accuracy. Dredze, Gevaryahu, and Bachrach (2007) proposed fast classifiers by introducing Just in Time (JIT) feature extraction, which creates features at classification time as needed by the classifier. The work utilized both low level complex and high level simple features with Support Vector Machine (SVM) to achieve spam detection accuracy up to 97%.

A comprehensive solution that includes both server-side filtering and client-side detection may offer high detection accuracy as well as good performance (Gao, Choudhary and Gang, 2010). Gao, Choudhary and Gang (2010) utilized a non-negative sparsity induced similarity measure for cluster analysis of spam images on the server-side. As getting sufficient labeled images for supervised training is difficult in real cases, human intervention based active learning is adopted at client side to avoid erroneously discarding genuine messages. The global unsupervised cluster analysis of the image corpus is carried on the server side; while active learning atclient side guides the users to label only those images that are escaped from server side filtering. The authors stated an accuracy of 99% at the client-side using SVM.

Some algorithms are capable of classifying spam images into different predefined categories for e.g. Binary Filtering with Multi-Label Classification (BFMLC) (Cheng et al., 2010). BFMLC is capable of considering both filter-oriented binary classifications as well as multi-label classification based on user preferences. According to user preference settings on the client side, the specific spam images are delivered to individuals. The authors stated the average accuracy of 96.309% and classify spam images as predefined topics with the average precision of 89.42%.

Some authors proposed multi layer image spam filtering system in order to achieve a good tradeoff between detection accuracy as well as performance (Liu, Tsao and Lee, 2010). The system filters the image spam by analysing both the mail header and the image. The first layer of the system proposed in the work (Liu, Tsao and Lee, 2010), utilizes Bayesian Classifier on extracted header features. The escaped spam mails are processed further by second layer by first extracting the high-level features such as the file name, width, file size, aspect ratio, height, and image format and utilizing SVM classifier. Authors applied SVM classifier in order to minimize the impact of classification results, due to inconsistent number of samples available in each category. If the first two layers do not have a consistent result, the 3rd layer of the system makes the final decision by analyzing the low-level features of the image such as the color histogram and the color moment. The experimental results shows that most image spam mails are identified by the first layer and the accuracy rate of 94% is achieved for the whole system.

Besides machine learning techniques, probabilistic approach like Hidden Markov Model (HMM) is also used by some authors for image-based spam detection (Jaswal and Sood, 2013). The authors used the extracted stemming words from spam image dataset and then applied HMM of spam filters to detect all the spam images. HMM is a probabilistic method to model sequence of data. HMM can also be used either for classification of spam images within a bayesian framework; or for latent clustering of the of spam images using their parameters.

The problem with email spam filters is that sometimes a valid message may be blocked. Hence automatically blocking/rejecting mail that is classified as spam will not be useful. The detection techniques should allow user to read the spam email or delete the spam email. To ease the user, these messages can be sorted based on the high probability of non-spam email at the top of list, before providing the messages to the user. The detectors should only indicate spam probability or its degree of confidence for the spam message but should not delete them.

3.9. SUMMARY

This chapter describes various features related to color, shape, texture, metadata domain of image based spam. These features represent unique characteristics of image spam. There is a need to select optimal and more discriminative set of features, in order to improve the classifier response. Low level image features gives high classification accuracy but low recall ratio and also time intensive. Extracting high level image features is fast as compared to that of low level image features but they suffer from low recall ratio and low classification accuracy. The accuracy of Image spam detection techniques based on the textual features is bounded by the efficiency of OCR techniques used. Also extracting the text content using OCR techniques is time consuming task and thus cannot utilized effectively for real time heavily loaded email servers.

The chapter discussion also focus that image spam detection can be seen as a multi disciplinary area comprising of image analysis, machine learning techniques, and artificial intelligent techniques.

REFERENCES

Aradhye, H., Myers, G., & Herson, J. A. (2005). Image Analysis for Efficient Categorization of Image-based Spam E-mail. *Proceedings of 8th International Conference on Document Analysis and Recognition (ICDAR-2005)*, 914–918. doi:10.1109/ICDAR.2005.135

Basheer, A., Ismail, K., & Omar, A. (2011). Texture Analysis-Based Image Spam Filtering. *Proceedings of 6th International Conference on Internet Technology and Secured Transactions*, 288-293.

Cheng, H., Qin, Z., Fu, C., & Wang, Y. (2010). A novel spam image filtering framework with Multi-Label Classification. *Proceedings of International Conference on Communications, Circuits and Systems (ICCCAS-2010)*, 282-285.

Dredze, M., Gevaryahu, R., & Elias, B. A. (2007). Learning Fast Classifiers for Image Spam. *Proceedings of 4th International Conference on Email and Anti-Spam*.

Feng, H., Yang, X., Liu, B., & Jiang, C. (2011). A Spam Filtering Method Based on Multi-modal Features Fusion. *Proceedings of Seventh International Conference on Computational Intelligence and Security (CIS-2011)*, 421-426.

Francesco, G., & Carlo, S. (2008). Combining visual and textual features for filtering spam emails. *Proceedings of 19th International Conference on Pattern Recognition (ICPR-2008)*, 1-4.

Gao, Y., Choudhary, A., & Gang, H. (2010). A Comprehensive Approach to Image Spam Detection:From Server to Client Solution. *IEEE Transactions on Information Forensics and Security*, *5*(4), 826–836. doi:10.1109/TIFS.2010.2080267

He, P., Wen, X., & Zheng, W. (2009). A Simple Method for Filtering Image Spam. *Proceedings of 8th IEEE/ACIS International Conference on Computer and Information Science (ICIS-2009)*, 910–913. doi:10.1109/ICIS.2009.101

Jaswal, V., & Sood, N. (2013). Spam detection system using Hidden Markov Model. *International Journal of Advanced Research in Computer Science and Software Engineering*, *3*(7), 304–308.

Krasser, S., Yuchun, T., Gould, J., Alperovich, D., & Judge, P. (2007). Identifying Image Spam based on Header and File Properties using C4.5 Decision Trees and Support Vector Machine Learning. *Proceedings of International Workshop on Information Assurance and Security Workshop (IAW-2007)*, 255-261. doi:10.1109/IAW.2007.381941

Lamia, M. K., Munesh, C., & Mohammadi, A. K. (2012). A Study of Image Spam Filtering Techniques. *Proceedings of Fourth International Conference on Computational Intelligence and Communication Networks (CICN-2012)*, 245-250.

Liu, Q., Zhang, F., Qin, Z., Wang, C., Chen, S., & Ma, Q. (2010). Feature selection for image spam classification. *Proceedings of International Conference on Communications, Circuits and Systems (ICCCAS-2010),* 294-297. doi:10.1109/ICCCAS.2010.5581994

Liu, T., Tsao, W., & Lee, C. (2010). A High Performance Image-Spam Filtering System. *Proceedings of Ninth International Symposium on Distributed Computing and Applications to Business, Engineering and Science (DCABES-2010),* 445-449. doi:10.1109/DCABES.2010.97

Mehta, B., Nangia, S., Gupta, M., & Nejdl, W. (2008). Detecting Image Spam using Visual Features and Near Duplicate Detection. *Proceedings of 17th International Conference on World Wide Web. (www2008),* 497–506. doi:10.1145/1367497.1367565

Peizhou, H., Xiangming, W., Wei, Z., & Xinqi, L. (2008). Filtering Image Spam Using File Properties and Color Histogram. *Proceedings of International Conference on Multimedia and Information Technology,* 276-279.

Peng, W., & Minoru, U. (2012). Spam Detection Using Sobel Operators and OCR. *Proceedings of 26th International Conference on Advanced Information Networking and Applications Workshops (WAINA-2012),* 1017-1022.

Soranamageshwari, M., & Meena, C. (2011). A Novel Approach towards Image Spam Classification. *International Journal of Computer Theory and Engineering, 3*(1), 84–88. doi:10.7763/IJCTE.2011.V3.287

Soranamageswari, M., & Meena, C. (2010). Histogram based image Spam Detection using Back Propagation Algorithm, *Global. Journal of Computer Science and Technology, 9*(5), 62–67.

Uemura, M., & Tabata, T. (2008). Design and Evaluation of a Bayesian-filter-based Image Spam Filtering Method. *Proceedings of 2nd International Conference on Information Security and Assurance (ISA-2008),* 46–51. doi:10.1109/ISA.2008.84

Wang, C., Zhang, F., Li, F., & Liu, Q. (2010). Image Spam Classification based on Low-level Image Features. *Proceedings of the International Conference on Communications, Circuits and Systems (ICCCAS-2010)*, 290-293.

Woods, N. C., Longe, O. B., & Roberts, A. B. C. (2012). A Sobel Edge Detection Algorithm Based System for Analyzing and Classifying Image Based Spam. *Journal of Emerging Trends in Computing and Information Sciences*, *3*(4), 506–511.

Xu, C., Chen, Y., & Chiew, K. (2010). An Approach to Image Spam Filtering Based on Base64 Encoding and N-Gram Feature Extraction. *Proceedings of 22nd International Conference on Tools with Artificial Intelligence (ICTAI-2010)*, 171-177. doi:10.1109/ICTAI.2010.31

Zhang, C., Chen, W., Chen, X., Tiwari, R., Yang, L., & Warner, G. (2009). A Multimodal Data Mining Framework for Revealing Common Sources of Spam Images. *Journal of Multimedia*, *4*(5), 313–320. doi:10.4304/jmm.4.5.313-320

Chapter 4

Image Spam Filters Based on Optical Character Recognition (OCR) Techniques

ABSTRACT

In 2003, the first image with the spam text inside was reported by Graham-Cumming. Later, this technique was utilized successfully by spammers, by sending image spam as MIME attachments instead of sending as simple image tags. The previous content filtering techniques based on text analysis of subject and body fields of email were ineffective to handle this new spam attack type. The first attempts made by researchers to detect such spam were based on Optical Character Recognition (OCR) methods. These methods tried to extract the spam texts/words from image spam and compare with existing spam text keyword database. This chapter provides the details of OCR methods, a literature review on spam filters based on OCR methods and their limitations.

4.1. OPTICAL CHARACTER RECOGNITION (OCR): INTRODUCTION

Optical Character Recognition (OCR) is a pattern recognition technique which involves the process of converting the printed/typed or handwritten text (usually in the form of images) into machine-encoded text. Figure 1 shows the simple block diagram of OCR Reader.

DOI: 10.4018/978-1-68318-013-5.ch004

Figure 1. OCR Reader

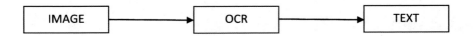

In data entry applications like passport documents, invoices, bank statements, computerized receipts, this technique is widely adopted. This method of digitizing printed texts helps to edit electronically the converted text and hence in turn, offers benefits like ease of searching, storing data in compact form, ease of displaying data on-line etc.

4.1.1. History

The history of OCR can be traced all the way back to 1809, when reading devices for the blind or telegraph applications were developed. In 1914, Emanuel Goldberg developed a machine to convert printed characters into standard telegraph code. Concurrently, Edmund Fournier developed a handheld scanner called Optophone, which can produce tones corresponding to the specific letters/characters in the printed document (Herbert, 1982, Dalbe, 1914). In the late 1920s, Emanuel Goldberg developed an optical code recognition system for searching microfilm archives. In 1950s, US Department of Defense created GISMO, a device that could read Morse Code as well as words on a printed page, one character at a time. In 1974, Ray Kurzweil developed omni-font OCR reading machine for the blind, which could recognize text printed in virtually any font. This device utilized the CCD flatbed scanner and the text-to-speech synthesiser. Later commercial version of the OCR computer programs were launched in the market for commercial purposes like uploading legal paper and news documents onto online databases. In the early 1990's, it was used by libraries for historic newspaper digitization projects. An open source GUI frontend PrintToBraille tool (Rose, 2009). was developed by A. G. Ramakrishnan and his team at Medical intelligence and language engineering lab, Indian Institute of Science, to convert scanned images of printed books to Braille books. In the 2000s, WebOCR – an online OCR tool was made available in a cloud computing environment and in mobile applications. Currently, many commercial open source OCR systems are available that support other language writing systems.

4.1.2. Applications

OCR engines are used for the following applications prominently:

1. **Data Entry:** It is widely used for data entry in business documents such as passport, check, invoice, bank statement, receipt, etc.
2. **Information Extraction:** It has proved its worth in insurance sector by extracting important / key information from information documents.
3. **Business Card Information Extraction:** Business sector is using it for creating the contact list of the card information.
4. **Textual Version of Printed Documents:** Textual versions of the printed documents eg book scanning are quickly generated by this technique.
5. **Electronic Image:** Formation of electronic images of searchable printed documents, like Google Books is carried out by this technique.
6. **Assistive Technology:** It is used to make the assistive technology for blind and visually impaired users.

4.1.3. Types of OCR

The OCR techniques can be categorized as optical character or word recognition techniques based on if one character or one word is processed at a time for targeted typewritten text. The techniques are also categorized as intelligent character or word recognition, usually based on the use of machine learning techniques. These intelligent techniques can process handwritten print script or cursive text both. The character, word, line OCR output can be understood with the help of the Figure 2. During pre-processing, the digital image is decomposed into its smallest component parts like text blocks, sentence/line blocks, word blocks and character blocks by discarding remaining unwanted components, such as lines, graphics, photographs etc. OCR techniques can be based on offline or online recognition. In offline recognition, an image or scanned document acts as a source while in case of online recognition, the successive points as a function of time and order of strokes act as source input.

Figure 2. OCR output blocks

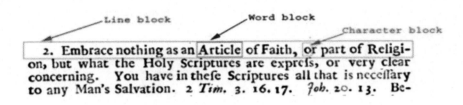

4.1.4. Factors Affecting OCR

The accuracy of OCR techniques depends on the many factors like quality of scanned/printed/handwritten document, scanning resolution, file format, bit depth of image, quality of source, algorithm, page layout, in-built dictionaries and pattern images used in OCR software (Rose, 2009). In order to improve the accuracy, cleanest/original version of hard copies should be used. The scanning resolution should be 300 dpi or above to capture as much image information and the file format should be lossless like .tiff. Scanning the images as greyscale, use of image optimisation methods to increase contrast/density, de-skewing pages so that word lines are horizontal, smoothing/rounding/sharpening character edges can further increase the accuracy of detection. Finally, selecting good OCR software containing rich database of pattern images and in-built dictionaries also matters for accuracy in detection.

4.1.5. Measuring OCR Accuracy Rates

OCR software calculates a confidence level for each character it detects, but it cannot tell if any character is correct or not. It can only specify it's confidence level in interpreting that character. Hence, some applications may need manual proofreading the converted documents and comparing it with OCR output. However such methods are very time consuming.

4.1.6. Advantages and Disadvantages of OCR

The comparisons of advantages and disadvantages of OCR are as given in Table 1.

Table 1. Pros and Cons of OCR

Advantages of OCR	Disadvantages of OCR
Cheaper than manual text detection, especially when large amounts of text detection is involved.	Accuracy depends on many parameters and hence cannot achieve 100% accuracy.
Much faster than manual text detection	All documents need manual verification of converted text for alignment, layout etc.
The latest software can recreate tables and/or the original layout.	In case of poor quality original document or textured background, more errors will result in interpreting text.
Cost effective technique when large amounts of text conversion is involved.	Costly technique when small amounts of text conversion are needed.

4.2. APPLICATIONS OF OCR TECHNIQUES IN IMAGE SPAM DETECTION

Various researchers have developed their image spam schemes based on OCR methods. Image spam detection techniques that are based on OCR methods, first extracts the embedded text in the spam/natural images and applies traditional text-based methods to filter the spam. The outputs of OCR are compared to some specific keywords or texts which are generally used in the spam emails. These OCR based methods also referred as content based spam filtering methods. The datasets used and the results achieved by these research works are presented in Table 1.

Many research works have been already carried out for extraction of text regions from images. These works tried to exploit the distinctive properties of text in terms of frequency and orientation information. Generally, text characters of the same string appear close to each other and are of similar height, orientation and spacing. This property is called as spatial cohesion and is commonly exploited using edge and connected component features of text characters.

OCR based image spam detection techniques are divided broadly into two categories.

1. **Keyword Based Detection:** A databank of keywords which are generally available in the spam emails is made and the output of the OCR is checked against these keywords (Sanz, HidalgoGomez, and PérezCortizo, 2008). These methods are easy to implement and require less processing time. However, they require frequent updating of database. Further, OCR techniques are computationally demanding and can easily be fooled by image artefacts or obfuscating techniques such as misspelling the keywords, scaling, rotation, translation and noise addition. High false positives may occur as presence of even a single keyword can label the mail as spam. To overcome the OCR errors and to reduce false positives, a rule can be set such that higher the number of keywords found means higher the chance of an image to be spam (Byun et al., 2007).

2. **Text Categorization:** In these techniques, the text extracted from the non-obfuscated images is used to label the mail as spam or ham. In present scenarios, wherein the spammers use various obfuscation techniques, this technique may not yield reliable results.

4.3. PREVIOUS WORK

This section provides a detailed literature review on existing image spam detection schemes based on OCR methods.

In order to reduce the computational complexity exhibited by OCR based filtering methods, Fumera, Pillai, and Roli (2006) proposed a hierarchical architecture for spam filter. The system will extract and analyze the text embedded in images using OCR with commercial software, ABBYY FineReader 7.0 Professional, only if previous low complex modules which analyze subject and body fields were not able to classify reliably email as shown in Figure 3.

Figure 3. Scheme proposed by (Fumera, Pillai, and Roli, 2006)

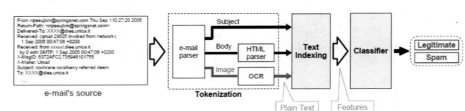

To reduce the complexity further, the authors also deployed image signatures along with text extracted. The image signature is easily available during classification phase to analyze image with same signature. The main limitations of the scheme stated are; use of legitimate email dataset is ignored during training phase, the OCR software used in this scheme is not optimized for spam detection application and hence, the scheme is ineffective in case if spammers used content obscuring techniques to images.

Biggo et al. (2007) proposed an approach to detect various obfuscating techniques used by the spammers, such as character breaking, merging, or introducing the noise like small dots in the image text region etc (Biggio et al., 2007). The presence of any obfuscating techniques used in an image indicates that an image is likely to be spam. Although these features were not capable of detecting the spam images independently but are good means of discriminating the low level characteristic of embedded text. The author measures the extent of the defects caused due to such obfuscating techniques on binarized image. The similar kinds of measures (such as degraded/broken/merged characters) are also used in assessing the performance of OCR methods. The author used demo version of commercial software ABBYY FineReader

Table 2.

Technique	Features	Dataset	Feature Selection	Total Number of Features	Classifier	Accuracy
(Fumera, Pillai, & Roli, 2006)	Subject, Body, Image Text extracted using OCR	SpamArchive corpus, Enron data set, Personal	Information Gain criterion	upto 20,000 features	SVM	80% (approx.)
(Wu et al., 2005).	Image Features- Banner and graphic feature, Embedded-text feature extraction, Position-Independent Features (PIF) Local Edge-Pattern (LEP), Local Edge-Density (LED), and Global Edge-Density (GED), Image location features	SpamArchive, Ling-Spam dataset		Upto 509	One class/ two class SVM	80% (approx.)
(Aradhye et al., 2005)	Extent of text feature, Color saturation features, Color heterogeneity features	Personal Spam1 Spam2 dataset		5	SVM	80% (approx.)

7.0 Professional for binarization of image. The results were not disclosed in the work; however the idea of detecting the presence of such techniques can be exploited for detecting the spam images.

In the same year, a SVM based spam detection model was proposed by Phuong and Tu (2007), which utilized scale and translation invariant features such as Edge Direction (ED) (Jain and Vailaya, 1996, Jain and Vailaya, 1998) and Edge Orientation Autocorrelogram (EOAC) (Mahmoudi et al., 2003) for representing the shape of an image. The global shape information was represented by the ED whereas correlation among the embedded text elements was represented by EOAC. The method computes a vector of similarity scores between spam image and a set of templates that contained only text is calculated for comparison. An accuracy of more than 80% was stated the authors. Also, in this method computationally intensive text recognition and image processing steps are avoided in order to make the detection fast.

Wan et al., (2008) designed a classifier which uses Color Roberts edge detector and a four stage Edge Classification-Based Text Localization (ECTL) algorithm (Zhang and Pan, 2001). ECTL extract text regions in four stages namely, edge detection (ED), corner detection CD), edge classification (EC), and candidate text regions refinement (CTRR). Total numbers of 47 features were used to distinguish text edges and non-text edges in an image. In CTRR nearby edges were merged together to form a cluster for achieving better accuracy. Color edge detector (CED) in place of ED was utilized for color images. Text regions were extracted with the accuracy of 97.6% for simple background and 94.9% for the complex background images. ECTL can be utilized in place of OCR technique for building a classifier.

In the same year, Francesco and Carlo (2008) used both visual and textual based features for spam detection. The textual based features extracted using this OCR based technique includes features like number of characters, number of words, ambiguity - ratio between the number of special and normal characters, correctness -ratio between the number of words that do not contain special characters and the number of words that contain special characters, special length - maximum length of a continuous, sequence of special characters, special distance - maximum distance between two special characters. Figure 4 (a)-(c) shows the distribution of number of characters, number of words and ambiguity in both spam and ham images.

Using OCR affects the speed and accuracy of detection, but adoption of both visual and text-based features can improve the performance.

Figure 4. Distribution of Number of Characters, Number of Words and Ambiguity

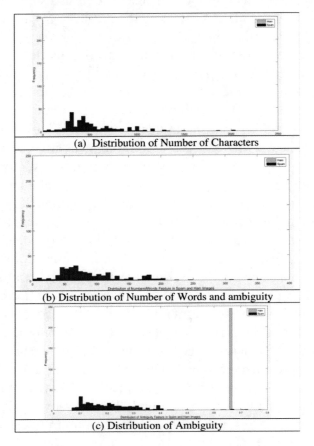

(a) Distribution of Number of Characters

(b) Distribution of Number of Words and ambiguity

(c) Distribution of Ambiguity

In 2009, Visual bag-of-words (VBOG), SVM and Tesseract-OCR were used by Hsia and Chen (2009) to build a classifier. Spam images have more text area as compared to ham images. Therefore, if the text area is more than some threshold value (set to 15% by the authors after analyzing various spam images) then the image is considered as ham. SVM and Tesseract-OCR were used to categorize the value of text area and VBOG was also utilized for detection of objects in images. The authors stated an accuracy of 94% with their proposed model.

Greg et al. (2010), had extracted text from the spam images using OCR technique in order to generate image signatures which is used as one of the spam features. This feature along with other features extracted from header information, message body content and metadata are also used. Weights are assigned to these features using mathematical model such that features which are known to be a relatively better indicator of spam are given a relatively higher weight than other features. The combined weights are to decide the spam score value.

Sathiya, Divakar and Sumi (2011) designed an OCR based model named Partial Image Spam Inspector (PIMSI). The model comprises of two modules namely convert classification module (CM) and evaluation module (EM). CM extracts the embedded text in spam image and checks for similarity against the known keywords (such as casino, casinos, chat room, click here, doctor prescribed, etc.) CM also extracts image characteristics such as RGB colors, contrast, radian, brightness, etc. for classification. If the similarity ratio is equal or more than the three-fourth value than the image is considered as spam by EM module. The accuracy results are not declared and the efficacy of this scheme was not evaluated against any dataset.

Peng, and Minoru (2012) proposed both one layer and two layer model which utilized the edge feature-representing apparent change in brightness for classification. One layer model utilized standard vertical, horizontal and diagonal Sobel operator. The ratio of results by standard and diagonal Sobel operator was checked against the preset threshold to identify the spam. Multiple layer schemes utilized Sobel operators along with OCR for detection. Sobel operator first identifies only those images consisting embedded characters. Next in second stage, OCR is applied to these identified images only. An accuracy of 90% was reported by two layer model. The distribution of the edge feature for ham and spam images given in Chapter 3 of this book, shows a lot of overlapping which may affect detection accuracy largely. OCR filter and sobel filter both are vulnerable to manmade noise. Also single feature based analysis may not able to capture global characteristics of images; hence it may affect detection accuracy further.

Many other approaches were proposed in the same year. A multi layer spam detection model designed by Li and Kim (2012), is based on first layer Bayesian filter, second layer SVM classifier followed by OCR in the third layer. These layers are managed by a single control unit. Each layer utilizes distinct technique, starting with text classification at the top most layer followed by image processing and lastly OCR. To reduce the computational complexity involved, the upper layer invokes the bottom layer, when it is not able to make the decision independently. OCR based bottom most layer utilizes the services of the previous layers to make the decision. An accuracy of 95% is stated by the said scheme. Similarly, Yamakawa and Yoshiura (2012) have examined the ability of Tesseract-OCR – a free OCR software and licensed with the Apache 2.0 License, for image spam detection. Here, the Tesseract-OCR is trained specific spam words and hence this decreases the detection time and helps to recognize the limited words accurately. In case, if no spam words are detected from image, image is enlarged by certain scale and again OCR detection software tries to extract and match words from enlarged image with spam word database. The limited number of images as well as limited number of words chosen for training may reduce the computational cost but it may lead to misclassification. The accuracy of 66.7% was stated in this model. Fadiora et al. (2012) employed pattern recognition techniques like grey scaling, edge detection and binarization in combination with OCR mechanism for image-based spams.

A model based on K-labels propagation model (KLPM), K-nearest neighbor (KNN) graph, label propagating process and utilizing scale and rotation invariant speeded up robust features (SURF) was proposed by the authors in the work (Qian et al., 2013) in 2013. Improved Means Clustering algorithm was used to normalize and to make various clusters of these features. A completely connected graph of these clusters was formed for classification. Results were carried out by using 90/10 rule (90% images for training and 10 for testing). To prove the efficacy of the KLPM the results were compared against Label Propagation Model (LPM) and Naive Bayesian Classifier (NBC). Accuracy of 95% was claimed against of 85% by NBC and 70% by LPM when 400 images were considered for testing.

In 2014, a Repetitive Pre-processing technique for Embedded Text Detection (ReP-ETD) was designed by the authors (Manek et al., 2014). Bag of word of 10 keywords including Viagra, browser, click, xanax, ciali, pill, price, address, type, ambien was prepared. Experiments were conducted using W-Random Forest, W-Random Tree, W-IBk, W-BIF Reader, K-NN, SVM, Naïve Bayes and linear SVM independently. An accuracy of 86.83% was stated using W-Random Forest and W-Random Tree. This approach requires frequent updation of bag of words as the detection results depends on keywords.

In the same year, Das and Vijay (2014) designed a stack based spam detection system similar to the work in (Georgios et al., 2001), which consists of OCR and SVM. The method exploits both embedded text extraction and low level features from spam image. The results are not declared by authors as the technique was not evaluated against any datasets. Similarly in the same year, Harisinghaney et al. (2014) suggested a spam detection method based on the frequency of the words which generally appears in spam images. The database of these words was prepared by extracting them by OCR technique.

Three different algorithms KN algorithm, Naïve Bayes algorithm and reverse DBSCAN algorithm were utilized to find the match of the extracted words against the database. If a match is found then the image is considered as spam. The author has introduced a database of white listed (based on the user choice irrespective of the type of the mail they send) web pages and domains which complements the black listed database (JWSPAMSPY, 2017). If the mail comes from the white list, then only it is passed directly to the user otherwise, the mail is considered as spam. The accuracy of 87% was achieved with Naïve Bayes algorithm, thus outperforming the other two algorithms. Also the Youn and Hyun-chong (2014) proposed a hierarchal model named SPONGY (SPamONtoloGY) for filtering text and image spam (Youn, & Hyun-chong, 2014). The extraction of embedded text is carried out by using all three types of the OCR techniques (The JOCR, 2016), (The Simple OCR, 2016) and (ASPRISE, 2016). Best results were obtained with Asprise OCR. This model requires the input in the RDF file format (The RDF, 2016). The combination of C4.5 Decision trees, RDF and Jena (APACHEJENA, 2016) was used to make the SPONGY architecture. The output of the C4.5 is mapped to RDF and the RDF output is fed to Jena to create ontology. The advantages of both globally trained and personally trained filters are combined in this two level filtering system. The authors stated the accuracy of 95% with this proposed model.

In 2015, a spam detection method based on the probability of words available in header and body of mail was suggested Chopra and Gaikwad (2015) and the scheme is capable of detecting both text as well as image spam. Here, OCR technique was used to extract the words embedded in spam image and these words acts as input to Naïve Bayes classifier for identifying spam words. A mail is considered as spam, if the detection probability is more than a predefined threshold. The accuracy of the proposed method is not mentioned by the author in his work. Also the authors safely assume the high accuracy by OCR module for extraction of embedded text from spam images, which may not be the case in case of obfuscated image spam. Similarly, Bansod, Mangrulkar, & Bhujade (2015) proposed OCR based spam detection based on the weights assigned to the frequently appearing spam and ham words in both text and image spam in the same year. Black Listing and White listing method is used during preliminary analysis such that If sender email id belongs to a domain that matches from the black list, then mail is predicted as spam without any further processing. Next, text is extracted directly from the content of mail in case text based spam. In case of image spam, OCR technique is used to extract text content. The extracted data is pre-processed using stemming process which may include removing suffixes like –ing, -ed, removing high frequency words like a, an, the, removing stop words etc. Next based on probability of words, corresponding weights (+ve for spam words or –ve for nonspam words) for words are determined. Artificial neural network is trained for the selected words and used for further classification. Spam assassin dataset of 500 mails having mixture of spam and non-spam mails and spam archives dataset having 700 spam images is used by the authors.

Currently, SpamAssassin, a commercial open-source spam filter (ApacheSpamAssassin, 2009) is available in public domain which offers a plug-in that can analyze the text embedded into images using OCR methods. If more than one keyword among a given specific set is detected in this extracted text, the message is termed as spam. The output decision is indicated by a boolean variable.

4.4. LIMITATIONS OF EXISTING OCR BASED SPAM DETECTION TECHNIQUES

To deal with spam images, researchers converted the images into the rich text format using OCR techniques and processed the extracted text using traditional text based filters. However, these detection techniques fail when the spammers obfuscate the text in image spam by adding noise, rotating texts etc. The spammers may also carry out highly unnoticeable changes like, shading the border or background, changing line spacing or margins, or adding tiny specks to the background etc. Spammers may also use Completely Automated Public Turing test to tell Computers and Humans Apart (CAPTCHA) methods to escape from OCR based detectors. CAPTCHA methods distort the original images by adding noisy backgrounds in such a way that only humans can identify the intended message (CAPTCHA, 2000). In general, CAPTCHA methods are used to protect free services from getting abused by automated scripts, to prevent dictionary attacks in password based authentication systems, and to hide email address from Web scrapers. But in case of image spam, the same CAPTCHA methods are exploited by spammers to get escaped from spam filters in order to abuse email users. It's true, technology is cursed with two faces pointing in opposite directions.

All such operations result in generation of a huge quantity of image spam containing random patterns with almost no repetitions and affect the quality

Table 3. Existing OCR based spam detection techniques: Comparison

Work	Classifier and Technique Used	Data Set	Results (%)
Biggio et al., (2007)	Parametric Complexity & Noise	Spam archive & Personal	---
Harisinghaney et al., (2014)	OCR & Naïve Bayes	Enron (Partial)	87
Chopra and Gaikwad (2015)	OCR & Naïve Bayes	Not Evaluated	---
Youn and Hyun-chong (2014)	Asprise OCR & SPONGY	Personal	95
Uemura and Tabata (2008).	Bayesian Filtering	Personal	90
Hsia and Chen (2009).	Tesseract-OCR & SVM	Spamarchive, Dredze	94
Wuy et al., (2005)	One & Two Class SVM	Dredze & Ling	81.40 - 99.93
Aradhye, Myers and Herson (2005)	Two-Class SVM	Google Images	73-87
Liu et al., (2010)	SVM	Spamarchive & Personal	97.90 - 98.60
Manek et al., (2014)	W-Random Forest, W-Random Tree, K-NN, SVM, Naïve Bayes & Linear SVM	ISH, Dredze,Trec07 & Personal	45.26 - 86.83
Peng and Minoru (2012)	OCR & Sobel Operators	Internet Collection	90
Li and Kim, (2012)	OCR, Bayesian & SVM	RPA, CSDMC, Hunter & Personal	79.90 - 95
Yamakawa and Yoshiura, (2012)	Tesseract-OCR	Personal	66.70
Sathiya, Divakar and Sumi, (2011).	OCR	Not Evaluated	---
Phuong and Minh, (2007)	SVM	Personal, Corel & Google Images	>=80
Wan et al., (2008)	Edge Classification Based Text Localization	Dredze	97.60
Qian et al., (2013)	K-Labels Propagation Model (Using K-Nearest Neighbor)	Dredze	95
Das and Vijay, (2014)	OCR & SVM	Not Evaluated	---

of the OCR output greatly, making spam detection difficult. Hence, spam images may get bypassed by the spam filters that are based on exact hash signature. The traditional content or signature based filtering based image spam detection techniques tend to fail against such manipulated images.

Further, OCR based image spam detection techniques are highly computationally intensive; hence not suitable for online/real time server side spam detection applications. Further, the accuracy of these techniques depends on various stated parameters. Many existing OCR techniques can only handle text against a plain monochrome background and cannot extract text from a complex or textured background. Spammers use obscuring techniques to prevent the OCR software from extracting any meaningful text for further analysis. Further, the accuracy also varies depending on their inbuilt text detectors. Hence, using computationally intensive OCR based detection methods may not be feasible for heavily loaded email servers.

4.5. SUMMARY

This chapter provides the detailed overview of OCR method and a thorough literature review on spam filters based on OCR methods. Since the text data is embedded in spam images in different font styles, sizes, orientations, colors, and against a complex background, the problem of extracting the candidate text region becomes a challenging one. The chapter brings out the limitations of existing spam detection techniques based on OCR methods to handle image based spam. Finally it provides the detailed comparison of these techniques. The major limitations in existing research works based on OCR methods suggests exploring other image features for detection and combining other techniques to detect image spam robustly. To restrict the motives of the spammers, the detection system can be developed robust enough not to get defeated by spammers easily. This indirectly may force spammers to use more complicated, sophisticated and costly techniques for producing spam images. To overcome the limitations of OCR based detection techniques, non-content based email spam filtering techniques are introduced by various researchers, details of which will be covered in the next chapters of this book.

REFERENCES

Apache Spam Assassin. (2009). *OCR Plugin*. Available from: http://wiki.apache.org/spamassassin/OcrPlugin

Apache Jena. (2016). *A Free and Open Source Java Framework for Building Semantic Web and Linked Data Applications*. Available from: http://jena.sourceforge.net/

Aradhye, H., Myers, G., & Herson, J. A. (2005). Image Analysis for Efficient Categorization of Image-based Spam E-mail. *Proceedings of 8th International Conference on Document Analysis and Recognition (ICDAR-2005)*, 914–918.

Asprise. (2017). *Asprise OCR and Barcode Recognition*. Available from: http://asprise.com/product/ocr/selector.php

Bansod, Mangrulkar, & Bhujade. (2015). Spam Classification using Artificial Neural Network with Weight Measures. *International Journal of Advanced Computer Technology*, *4*(6), 68–72.

Biggio, B., Fumera, G., Pillai, I., & Roli, F. (2007). Image Spam Filtering using Visual Information. *Proceedings of 14th International Conference on Image Analysis and Processing*, 105-110. doi:10.1109/ICIAP.2007.4362765

Byun, B., Lee, C. H., Webb, S., & Pu, C. (2007). A Discriminative Classifier Learning Approach to Image Modeling and Spam Image Identification. *Proceedings of 4th Conference on Email and Anti-Spam, (CEAS-2007)*.

CAPTCHA. (2000). *The CAPTCHA Project*. Available from: http://captcha.net

Chang, C. C., & Lin, C. J. (2001). *LibSVM: A Library for Support Vector Machines*. Available from: https://www.csie.ntu.edu.tw/~cjlin/libsvm/

Chopra, N., & Gaikwad, K. P. (2015). Image and Text Spam Mail Filtering. *International Journal of Computer Technology and Electronics Engineering*, *5*(3), 15–18.

Dalbe, E. E. F. (1914). On a Type-Reading Optophone. *Proceedings - Royal Society. Mathematical, Physical and Engineering Sciences*, *90*(619), 373–375. doi:10.1098/rspa.1914.0061

Das, M., & Vijay, P. (2014). Analysis of an Image Spam In Email Based On Content Analysis. *International Journal on Natural Language Computing*, *3*(3), 129–140. doi:10.5121/ijnlc.2014.3313

Fadiora, B., Wada, F., & Longe, O. B. (2012). Combining Optical Character Recognition (OCR) and Edge Detection Techniques to Filter Image-Based Spam E-Mails. *African Journal of Computing and ICT*, *5*(1), 59–68.

Francesco, G., & Carlo, S. (2008). Combining Visual and Textual Features for Filtering Spam Emails. *Proceedings of 19th International Conference on Pattern Recognition (ICPR-2008)*, 1-4.

Georgios, S., Androutpoulos, I., Paliouras, G., Vangelis, K., Spyropoulos, C. D., & Stamatopoulos, P. (2001). Stacking Classifiers for Anti-spam Filtering of E-mails. *Proceedings of 6th Conference on Empirical Methods in Natural Language Processing (EMNLP-2001)*, 44–50.

Giorgio, F., Pillai, I., & Fabio, R. (2006). Spam Filtering based on the Analysis of Text Information Embedded into Images. *Journal of Machine Learning Research*, 7, 2699–2720.

Greg, W., Yanyan, Y., Scott, P., & Steven, L. (2010). *Message stream analysis for spam detection and filtering.* United States Patent No.: US 7,716,297 B1.

Harisinghaney, A., Dixit, A., Gupta, S., & Arora, A. (2014). Text and Image Based Spam Email Classifiation using KNN Naive Bayes and Reverse DBSCAN Algorithm. *Proceedings of International Conference on Reliability, Optimization and Information Technology (ICROIT-2014)*, 153-155.

Herbert, F. S. (1982). *The History of OCR, Optical Character Recognition.* Manchester Center: Recognition Technologies Users Association.

Hsia, J., & Chen, M. (2009). Language-model-based Detection Cascade for Efficient Classification of Image-based Spam E-mail. *Proceedings of IEEE International Conference on Multimedia and Expo.(ICME-2009)*, 1182–1185.

Jain, A. K., & Vailaya, A. (1996). Image Retrieval using Color and Shape. *Pattern Recognition, Elsevier*, 29(8), 1233–1244. doi:10.1016/0031-3203(95)00160-3

Jain, A. K., & Vailaya, A. (1998). Shape-based Retrieval: A Case Study with Trademark Image Database. *Pattern Recognition, Elsevier*, 31(9), 1369–1390. doi:10.1016/S0031-3203(97)00131-3

JOCR. (2016). *GOCR: The Open Source Character Recognition.* Available from: http://jocr.sourceforge.net/links.html

JWSPAMSPY. (2017). *Spam Domain Blacklist.* Available from: http://www.joewein.de/sw/blacklist.htm

Li, X. M., & Kim, U. M. (2012). A Hierarchical Framework for Content-based Image Spam Filtering. *Proceedings of 8th International Conference on Information Science and Digital Content Technology (ICIDT-2012)*, 149-155.

Liu, Q., Qin, Z., Cheng, H., & Wan, M. (2010). Efficient modeling of spam images. Proceedings of 3rd International Symponium on Intelligent Information Technology and Security Informatics (IITSI-2010), 663–666. doi:10.1109/IITSI.2010.40

Mahmoudi, F., Shanbehzadeh, J., Amir-Masoud, E., & Soltanian-Zadeh, H. (2003). Image Retrieval based on Shape Similarity by Edge Orientation Autocorrelogram. *Pattern Recognition, Elsevier*, *36*(8), 1725–1736. doi:10.1016/S0031-3203(03)00010-4

Nhung, N. P., & Phuong, T. M. (2007). An Efficient Method for Filtering Image-Based Spam. *Proceedings of IEEE International Conference on Research, Innovation and Vision for the Future*, 96-102. doi:10.1109/RIVF.2007.369141

Peng, W., & Minoru, U. (2012). Spam Detection Using Sobel Operators and OCR. *Proceedings of 26th International Conference on Advanced Information Networking and Applications Workshops (WAINA-2012)*, 1017-1022.

Qian, X., Zhang, W., Zhang, Y., & Zhou, G. (2013). Detecting Image Spam Based on K-Labels Propagation Model. *Proceedings of 10th Web Information System and Application Conference*, 170-175. doi:10.1109/WISA.2013.40

RDF. (2014). *Resource Description Framework*. Available from: https://www.w3.org/2001/sw/wiki/RDF

Rose, H. (2009). How good can it get? Analyzing and Improving OCR accuracy in Large Scale Historic Newspaper Digitisation Programs. *D-Lib Magazine, 15*(3/4). Available from: http://www.dlib.org/dlib/march09/holley/03holley.html

Sanz, E. P., Hidalgomez, J. M., & Perezcortizo, J. C. (2008). *Email Spam Filtering. In Advances in Computers* (Vol. 74, pp. 45–114). Elsevier.

Sathiya, V., Divakar, M., & Sumi, T. S. (2011). Partial Image Spam E-mail Detection using OCR. *International Journal of Engineering Trends and Technology, 1*(1), 55–59.

SIMPLEOCR. (2016). *Simple Software: Simple Solutions for Document Management*. Available from: http://www.simpleocr.com/

TEACHICT. (2017). *Optical Character Recognition*. Available from: http://www.teach-ict.com/as_a2_ict_new/ocr/AS_G061/312_software_hardware/input_devices/miniweb/pg12.htm

Uemura, M., & Tabata, T. (2008). Design and Evaluation of a Bayesian-filter-based Image Spam Filtering Method. *Proceedings of 2nd International Conference on Information Security and Assurance (ISA-2008)*, 46–51. doi:10.1109/ISA.2008.84

Wan, M., Zhang, F., Cheng, H., & Liu, Q. (2008). Text Localization in Spam Image using Edge Features. *Proceeding of International Conference on Communications, Circuits and System (ICCCAS-2008)*, 838-842.

Wu, C., Cheng, K., Qiang, Z., & Wu, Y. (2005). Using Visual Features for Anti-Spam Filtering. *Proceedings of International Conference on Image processing (ICIP-2005)*.

Yamakawa, D., & Yoshiura, N. (2012). Applying Tesseract-OCR to Detection of Image Spam Mails. *Proceedings of 14th Asia-Pacific Network Operations and Management Symposium. (APNOMS-2012)*, 1-4. doi:10.1109/APNOMS.2012.6356068

Youn, S., & Hyun-Chong, C. (2015). Improved Spam Filter via Handling of Text Embedded Image E-mail. *Journal of Electronics Engineering Technolgy*, *10*(1), 401–407. doi:10.5370/JEET.2015.10.1.401

Zhang, Y., & Pan, V. (2001). Design of a New Color Edge Detector for Text Extraction under Complex Background. *Journal of Software*, *12*, 1229–1235.

Chapter 5

Near Duplicate Detection–Based Image Spam Filters

ABSTRACT

A picture is worth a thousand words. Spam images give us many hints; one of them is that they are duplicates. Spam images are often generated from the same templates (which are designed by spammers) as they are sent to various recipients at the same time in batches. Various spam images are generated by randomization of the contents of these templates; as a result a similarity or uniqueness is present among the spam images. This similarity property in visually similar spam images can be exploited by the spam detectors for discriminating them from ham. The spam detectors can further trained on new data, if the spam images are generated from different templates, which is not a frequent phenomenon as it is resources intensive. The detection schemes that exploit the near duplicate characteristics of image spam, uses different types of image characteristics to calculate the similarity among spam images. This chapter provides the details of near duplicate detection based image spam filters, a literature review on these spam filters and their limitations.

DOI: 10.4018/978-1-68318-013-5.ch005

5.1. EXAMPLES OF SIMILAR IMAGES

Some of the examples of similar images which may be generated by spammers using different randomizing techniques are as follows.

5.1.1. Illustration Substitution

It means some of the illustrations are changed with some other illustrations and rest all the other things remains the same. It can be easily understood by the Figure 1 in which text matter in both the images are same, but the bunch of leaves at the top right corner is replaced by the ball of red ribbon. These two images are almost same only differs at the top right corner. The feature of these images differs very little due to the changes made by the spammer. So the technique based on near duplicate detection will easily detect these images made from the same base or template image.

5.1.2. Different Visual Features

It means visual features are changed with minor text changes rest all the other things remains the same. It can be easily understood by the Figure 2 in which the text matter in both the images are same with little variations, while images differs in visual at the left and the right side. The text changes

Figure 1. Spam images with illustration substitution

Figure 2. Spam images with almost identical text content but totally different visual features

are depicted by the red color while the visual features are marked by the blue color rectangles. So these two images are also made of the same base image.

5.1.3. Text and Background Color Changes

It means visual features are same but some of the words and their colors are changed. It can be easily understood by the Figure 3 given below in which words in both the images are differs. The changed words / sentences are depicted by the red colors. So these two images are also made of the same base image.

From these examples of similar images we can say, spammers tend to produce many small variations for a template image in order to circumvent simple signature-based anti-spam filters using different tricks like translation, rotation, scaling, local changes and adding random noises etc.

5.2. PREVIOUS WORK

Near duplicate spam detection methods exploit the uniqueness in the received spam images. These techniques are based on the assumption that, although spammers add randomization to the spam images generated from templates, they still want to deliver clear information to end users. At the same time,

Figure 3. Examples of word substitution, illustration alteration/replacement, text and background color changes

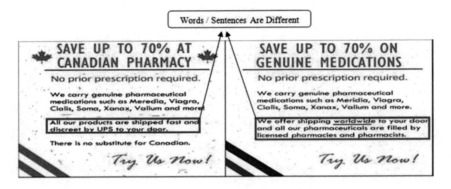

they want to use efficient methods to generate huge volume of unique spam images without obscuring the template image too much. Generally, a set of similar spam images with various minor changes implies a common origin of image spam.

The various datasets used and the results (range wherever applicable) achieved by works described below are presented in Table 1.

To achieve low false positives, the authors (Wang, 2007) exploited the similarity property in spam images using three filters namely, Color histogram, Harr wavelet, and Orientation histogram in the suggested model. Figure 4 and Figure 5 shows the proposed basic image spam detection system framework and the image spam filter respectively (Wang, 2007).

Initially, some of the images are captured by the traditional techniques (honey pots, dummy accounts) and then the filters are trained on the features

Table 1. Comparison of near duplicate detection algorithms

Work	Classifier and Technique Used	Data Set	Results (%)
Wang et al., (2007)	Color histogram, Harr wavelet & Orientation histogram	Corel, pbase.com, photo. net	83.30 - 100
He, Wen and Zheng (2009)	Gray and Colour histogram filter	Princeton, Bupticn, FHham	80.60 - 98.50
Qu and Zhang (2009).	Two class SVM	SpamArchieve, Personal	93.54
Hou et al., (2012).	Vocabulary tree	Dredze, Personal	99.50
Zhang et al., (2009).	Multimodal Clustering	Personal	97.20

Figure 4. Image spam detection system architecture

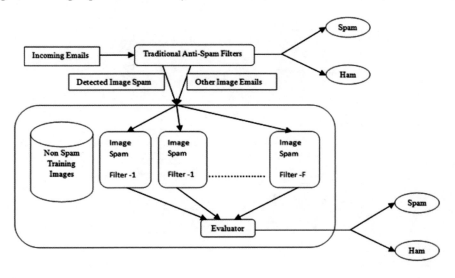

Figure 5. An image spam filter

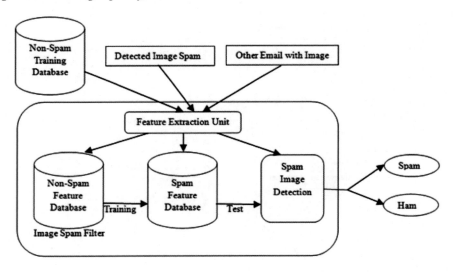

of these captured images to classify the new incoming images. Figure 6 (a)-(h) shows some of the sample spam images generated from same template, after applying different randomizing methods like shifting, change of URL, resize, text font change etc.

The L1 distance calculated between color histogram features of template spam image and other spam images (which are created from the same template)

Figure 6. Sample spam images created with same template spam image

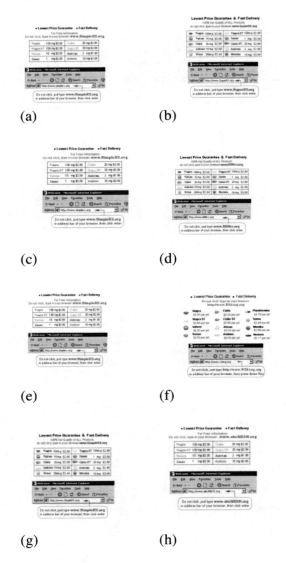

(a)

(b)

(c)

(d)

(e)

(f)

(g)

(h)

is minimum compared to that of other natural images. Similarly, the L1 distance calculated between Haar Wavlet or Orientation Histogram features of template spam image and other spam images (which are created from the same template) is very low compared to that of other natural images. Figure 7 shows the distribution of L1 distance of color histogram, Haar wavelet and orientation histogram features (Wang, 2007) between Selected Template spam

Figure 7. Distribution of L1 distance for (Wang, 2007) features between template spam image to natural images and template spam image to other spam images

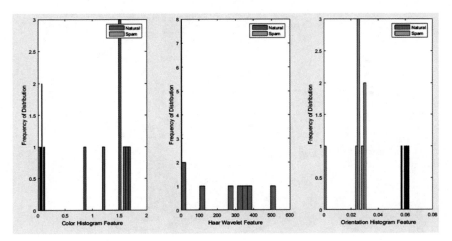

image and eight sample natural images and between Selected Template spam image and eight sample spam images which are created from same template. The distribution shows the demarcation and hence these features can be used for efficient spam detection.

The image were classified based on the outcome of the filters in three ways, i.e., 'AND', 'OR' and 'VOTE'. In AND method, image is considered as spam if the output of all the filters is same. In OR method, image was considered as spam if any filter designate it as spam. In VOTE method, image is considered as spam if the output of predefined number of filters is same. The authors stated that the best results were achieved by using Orientation histogram with lesser false positives. The results on various datasets give accuracy in the range of 83.3% to 100%. The major disadvantages of the scheme are as; selection of proper threshold is difficult, selection of AND, OR and Voting method affects the accuracy of spam detection as stated in the results given by author (Wang, 2007), finding the template image for received spam is difficult and the database need to be frequently updated for received different templates.

He, Wen and Zheng (2008) proposed FH algorithm which carries out filtering at two levels namely file properties discrimination (such as file size, width, height, and bit depth) in the first and histogram filtering (such as color or gray-level) in the second. Figure 8 shows the basic framework proposed by the author. In order to access the similarity among images the file

Figure 8. The architecture of FH algorithm

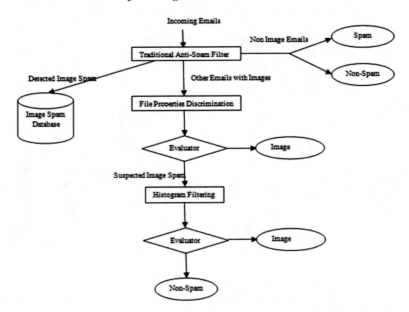

properties were compared to a predefined threshold. If similarity is noticed than classification based on histogram was carried out at second level. The results on various datasets fall within the range of 80.60% to 98.50%.

Later, a system based on two class SVM and using low level (color moments, texture, and shape) and high level characteristics for detecting near-duplicate was designed by Qu and Zhang (2009). Figure 9 and Figure 10 shows the architecture and feature extraction process of the proposed scheme. The low

Figure 9. Image spam system architecture

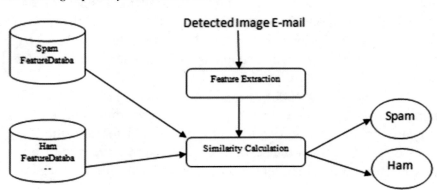

Figure 10. Process of features extraction

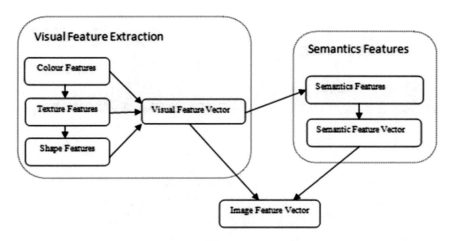

level and high level characteristics were compared with the two datasets (Spam and ham) for finding out the similarity. An accuracy of 93.54% was achieved by this model.

In 2009, Zuo et al., (2009) suggested use of Fourier-Mellin translation, scaling and rotation invariant descriptor to capture commonness in image spam. Caltech-256 corpus is used to create ham dataset while; SpamArchive and Dredze corpus is used to create spam dataset fo the experimentation. The Fourier-Mellin invariant matrix is extracted from each image in dataset and converted into a 1D vector by row concatenation. The Principal Components Analysis (PCA) is performed to reduce the dimension of features and a one-class SVM classifier is trained to classify spam images from ham. The precision rate, recall rate and F1 score stated are 98%, 80%, 89% approximately. The average time to classify an image is stated as 190 milliseconds. However the distribution of mean and variance of Fourier-Mellin descriptors are found to be more overlapping in case of spam and ham images in Dredze dataset (see Figure 11). This may affect accuracy of the detection. Also, as author has utilized single feature for spam detection; the scheme may suffer from accuracy.

In the same year, Zhang proposed a multimodal clustering algorithm for spam detection (Zhang et. al., 2009). Through clustering, spam images whose visual effects and/or textural contents resemble each other are grouped into clusters, revealing common origins of those images. Generally, spam images do not have continuous texture features and are produced as low resolution/

Figure 11. Distribution of mean and variance of Fourier-Mellin coefficients

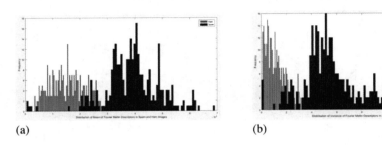

(a) (b)

poor quality images with many random noises. As readability is important for spam images, they will have sufficient background and foreground and background area will have more uniformity than foreground illustrations as shown in Figure 12 (a) and Figure 12 (b) respectively for two sample spam images. Spam image 2 differs from Spam image 1 by changing the text part slightly i.e. by addition of slight noise. In this work, spam image is segmented into text areas, foreground illustration areas, and background areas. To extract visual features, the authors construct color-code histograms of foreground

Figure 12. Foreground illustrations of sample spam images

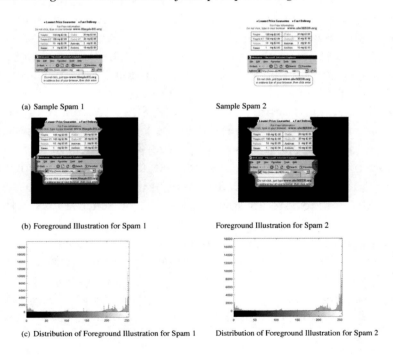

(a) Sample Spam 1 Sample Spam 2

(b) Foreground Illustration for Spam 1 Foreground Illustration for Spam 2

(c) Distribution of Foreground Illustration for Spam 1 Distribution of Foreground Illustration for Spam 2 illustrations as the color feature, use foreground illustration layout as another visual feature, and extract the texture features of foreground illustrations as the third visual feature. The proposed algorithm first calculates the image similarities in a pair-wised manner with respect to the visual features, and the images with similarities sufficiently high are grouped together. In the second level clustering, text clues are also considered. Further, a string matching method is used to compare the closeness of texts in two images, which is used as a criterion to refine the clustering results from the first level clustering.

Figure 12 (c) and Figure 12 (d) shows the distribution of intensities in foreground illustrations of corresponding spam images. Here, first background approximation image is obtained by removing all foreground object using morphological opening operation using a structuring element of size greater than that of text (disk-shaped structuring element with a radius of 25 in this example). The foreground illustrations are obtained after subtracting the background approximation image from original spam images and shows significant similarity. This fact is exploited in this algorithm. Subtraction of background noise may enhance the accuracy of clustering.

A multimodal technique which utilized conditional entropy technique to cluster spam images based on similarity and capable of finding their sources was proposed by Zhang et al., (2009). For clustering images were segmented into three areas which are text areas, foreground areas, background areas and similarity was establishing based on text and visual features (color, layout and texture) of these areas. Four clusters namely, text only, foreground illustrations, mixture of text and illustrations, neither illustrations nor text were formed and an accuracy of 97.2% was achieved.

In 2011, Wang et al., (2011) suggested near-duplicate image spam detection based on cross entropy. Although spammers try to introduce small variations in the template image to generate spam images, these variations may not be able to affect invariant regions. This technique tries to extract the local invariant features of spam using Speeded up Robust Features (SURF). The Figure 13 shows the distribution of one of the SURF Features –Metrics for ham and spam images.

To deal with high dimensional variable length features, Expectation Maximization (EM) is used to fit the parameters of the Gaussian Mixture Distribution (GMM) on extracted local invariant feature vectors. Using CE as the distance measurement between Gaussian distributions, performance of Kmeans algorithm to cluster the GMMs is improved. The precision of this method is given about 96%.

Figure 13. Distribution of SURF features–metrics

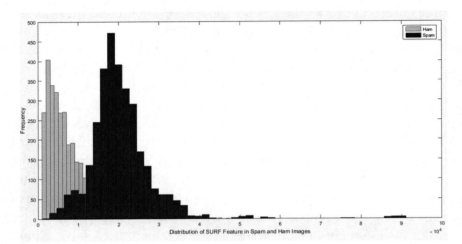

In 2012, Hou et al., (2012) suggested a model based on scalable vocabulary tree for detection for storing large spam database with false positive rate of less than 0.02%. Figure 14 shows the architecture of the proposed scheme. The method utilizes scale invariant feature based on sub-block color histogram and rotation invariant feature based on Oriented FAST and Rotated BRIEF (ORB) to deal with near duplicate property of spam images. Here, visual descriptor BRIEF is referred as Binary Robust Independent Elementary Features. Compared with Scale-invariant feature transform (SIFT) and Speeded Up Robust Features (SURF), ORB is a computationally-efficient. The scalable vocabulary tree enables extremely efficient retrieval and hence is chosen to create ORB feature index. The low time and storage complexity of using ORB descriptor makes it a good choice for real time massive spam data analysis. The authors stated low false positive rate and higher detection accuracy on spam dataset based on Dredze and SpamArchive Corpura. This method fails to detect spam with very few feature points and also it is required to update spam corpus periodically.

Figure 14. Near-duplicate Detection Scheme by Yixin (Yixin, 2012)

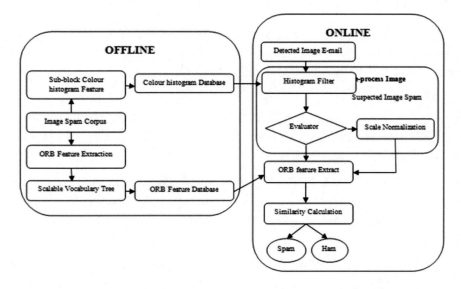

5.3. COMPARISON

Table 1. gives the detail comparison for all these schemes. It can be seen that, most of these schemes provide detection rate more than 90%.

All types of features are utilized in making the detection system. The efficiency in turn of processing time and robust characteristics can be achieved by making hierarchical model in which different features are utilized at different layers for identification.

5.4. SUMMARY

This chapter provides the detailed overview of spam detection methods based on near duplicate detection schemes. These techniques exploit the similarity property in visually similar spam images for discriminating spam from ham. The chapter also brings out the limitations of these spam detection techniques. Finally it provides the detailed comparison of these techniques.

REFERENCES

He, P., Wen, X., & Zheng, W. (2009). A Simple Method for Filtering Image Spam. *Proceedings of 8th IEEE/ACIS International Conference on Computer and Information Science (ICIS-2009)*, 910–913.

Hou, Y., Zhao, B., Zhang, H., & Yan, H. (2012). A Fast image spam filter based on ORB. *Proceedings of 3rd IEEE International Conference on Network Infrastructure and Digital Content (IC-NIDC 2012)*, 503-507. doi:10.1109/ICNIDC.2012.6418804

Nister, D., & Stewenius, H. (2006). Scalable Recognition with a Vocabulary Tree. *Proceedings of IEEE Computer Society Conference on Computer Vision and Pattern Recognition (CVPR- 2006)*, 2161-2168. doi:10.1109/CVPR.2006.264

Qu, Z., & Zhang, Y. (2009). Filtering Image Spam using Image Semantics and Near-duplicate Detection. *Proceedings of 2nd International Conference on Intelligent Computation Technology and Automation (ICICTA-2009)*, 600–603. doi:10.1109/ICICTA.2009.151

Rublee, E., Rabaud, V., Konolige, K., & Bradski, G. (2011). ORB: An Efficient Alternative to SIFT or SURF. *Proceedings of the International Conference on Computer Vision (ICCV-2011)*, 2564-2571. doi:10.1109/ICCV.2011.6126544

Wang, M., Zhang, W., & Zhang, Y. (2011). Detecting Image Spam Based on Cross Entropy. *Proceedings of the Eighth Web Information Systems and Applications Conference (WISA-2011)*, 19-22.

Wang, Z., Josephson, W., Lv, Q., Charikar, M., & Li, K. (2007). Filtering Image Spam with Near-duplicate Detection. *Proceedings of 4th International Conference on Email and Anti-spam (CEAS-2007)*.

Zhang, C., Chen, W., Chen, X., Tiwari, R., Yang, L., & Warner, G. (2009). A Multimodal Data Mining Framework for Revealing Common Sources of Spam Images. *Journal of Multimedia*, 4(5), 313–320. doi:10.4304/jmm.4.5.313-320

Zuo, H., Li, X., Wu, O., Hu, W., & Luo, G. (2009). Image Spam Filtering using Fourier-mellin Invariant Features. *Proceedings of International Conference on Acoustics, Speech, and Signal Processing (ICASSP-2009)*, 849–852.

Chapter 6
Visual Feature–Based Image Spam Filters

ABSTRACT

This chapter provides the details of visual feature based image spam filters, a literature review on these spam filters and their limitations. These methods are generally computationally efficient and exhibits more accuracy in presence of various noises compared to OCR based detection schemes, as they do not include any text recognition stage (Lamia et al., 2012). Previously discussed near-duplicate spam detection methods are likely to perform well in abstracting base templates, when given enough examples of various spam templates in use (Mehta et al., 2008). However, the generalization ability of these methods will be limited. Visual feature based spam detection methods are generally built using different high level and/or low level image features (refer Chapter 3 of this book) related to color, shape, texture characteristics of spam images; hence they have more generalization capability (Lamia et al., 2012). Mostly; these techniques exploit the text intensive and noisy nature of spam images.

6.1. PREVIOUS WORK

This section provides a detailed literature review of some good works proposed using image feature based techniques for spam detection.

Aradhye et al., (2005) exploits the text intensive nature of image spam by calculating 1) Extent of text feature - fraction of the total area of image that falls under text region, 2) Color Saturation Features - fraction of the

DOI: 10.4018/978-1-68318-013-5.ch006

total number of pixels in the image for which the difference max(R,G,B) – min(R,G,B) is greater than some threshold T (here, T=50 set) and 3) Color Heterogeneity Features. Figure 1 shows the distribution of Color Saturation Feature for both spam and ham images which shows good separable feature. However, no such good separation is observed in color heterogeneity feature. The authors claimed approximately 80% detection accuracy.

The method proposed by Nhung and Phuong (2007) uses computationally efficient edge based feature vector extraction to calculate vector of similarity (L1 distances) measures from an image to a small set of templates. Edge Directions (ED) and Edge Orientation Autocorrelogram (EOAC) are used as edge based translation and scale invariant features. ED is histogram of edge angles and reflects global shape information. Image spam's text intensive nature is exploited in this scheme, as text elements have special shape characteristics that differentiate them from that of background or other elements. Figure 2 (b) shows the output of edge detection using Sobel operator for sample spam image (See Figure 2 (a)).

The authors in this work have used SVM classifier in Weka Tool for experimentation on personal dataset only. Authors claim overall accuracy of 80% for the scheme. Using edge-based feature only may allow fast processing

Figure 1. Distribution of color saturation feature for spam and ham images

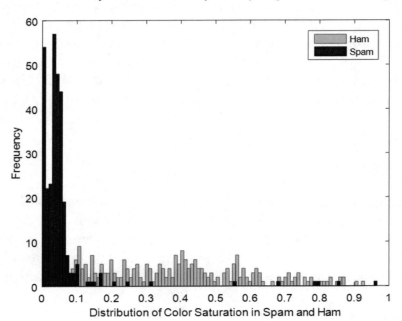

Figure 2. Edge direction feature for sample spam image

along with capturing regularities in shapes of text intensive spam images but may fail to achieve generalization capability.

In the same year, Byun et al., (2007) considered four spam image properties: color moment, color heterogeneity, conspicuousness, and self-similarity for image based spam detection (Byun et al., 2007). They applied multi-class characterization instead of single class characterization to improve detection robustness along with maximal figure-of-merit (MFoM) learning algorithm to design classifiers. Spam images are first categorized as text intensive synthetic/artificially modified images with diverse background region and non-synthetic/ images with no artificial modifications. Figure 3 (a)-(f) shows distribution of first and second order color moments in spam and ham images. The first order central moments shows wider separation compared to that of second order central moments here.

The authors calculated color heterogeneity, by first scaling image by the maximum possible intensity in the RGB channels and converting scaled image to an indexed image by using minimum variance quantization. The RMS error between the original image and the indexed image is used as color

Figure 3. Distribution of first and second order color moments in spam and ham images

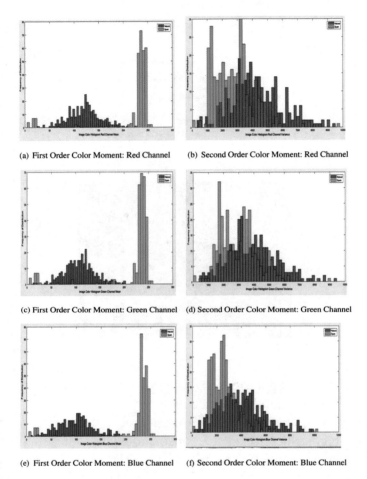

(a) First Order Color Moment: Red Channel   (b) Second Order Color Moment: Red Channel

(c) First Order Color Moment: Green Channel   (d) Second Order Color Moment: Green Channel

(e) First Order Color Moment: Blue Channel   (f) Second Order Color Moment: Blue Channel

heterogeneity feature which found no significant during our experiments; although natural images have more color heterogeneity and hence lower RMS errors than that of spam images. Calculation of conspicuousness feature - based on highly contrast property of spam images and self-similarity feature - based on uniform background property of spam images is highly computational. The authors claimed the detection rate of 81.5% and 5.6% of misclassification of legitimate images and good performance compared to the scheme discussed in the work (Aradhye et al., 2005).

In 2008, Mehta, Saurabh and Manish (2008) proposed two different approaches for image based spam detection; the results shows that the one based on visual features provides more accuracy than that based on near duplicate detection method. The authors exploit the image spam properties that; 1) Almost all image spam contains text messages, 2) they are usually noisy and made distinct from one another by carrying out different operations like rearranging, adding random noise, random patterns or borders, changing background, font, colors or fontsize etc. 3) Image spam use html messages such that text contained in I-spam images and the text contained in the HTML body usually have no correlation, 4) Natural images tend to have smoother distribution in RGB or LAB color-space than image spam and 5) Image spam are near-duplicates or template based. The authors here proposed color coherence vector which reflects the degree to which pixels of that color are members of large similarly-colored regions. Figure 4 shows the distribution of mean of total 128 color coherence feature vectors extracted from spam and ham images. Here each pixel is classified either coherent or incoherent depending on the size in pixels of its connected component; after blurring the image and discretizing the color space.

The authors suggested texture feature called autocorrelation which measures the coarseness of an image by evaluating the linear spatial relationships between texture primitives. Figure 5 (c) and Figure 5 (d) shows the 2D plot of autocorrelation feature extracted from sample ham image (see Figure 5 (a)) and spam image (see Figure 5 (b)) respectively. It can be seen that, for sample ham image, the autocorrelation function decreases rapidly with increasing distance in case of sample ham image whereas it decreases slowly with increasing distance in case of sample spam image.

Figure 4. Distribution of mean of total 128 color coherence feature vector

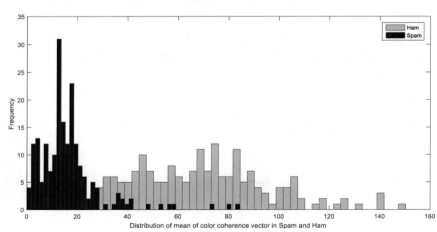

127

Figure 5. 2D Plot of autocorrelation feature of sample ham and spam image

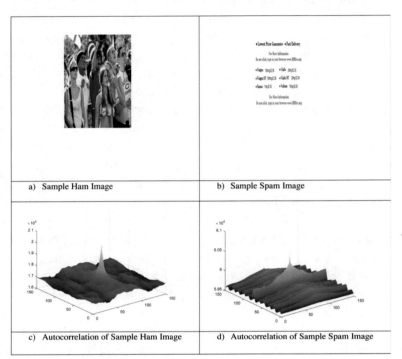

a) Sample Ham Image	b) Sample Spam Image
c) Autocorrelation of Sample Ham Image	d) Autocorrelation of Sample Spam Image

The author also suggested additional texture related features called 1) edge frequency which is inversely related to the autocorrelation function, 2) Primitive length (run length)- continuous set of maximum number of pixels in the same direction that have the same gray level and 3) Co-occurrence Matrices. Besides color and texture related features, the scheme also utilizes shape related features – central moments, eccentricity, Legendre and Zernike moments (Tahmasbi, Saki and Shokouhi, 2011). Figure 6 shows the distribution of eccentricity in both spam and ham images. Eccentricity is given by Equation (6.1).

$$Eccentricity = \frac{(\mu_{20} - \mu_{02})^2 + 4\mu_{11}\mu_{11}}{(\mu_{20} + \mu_{02})^2} \tag{6.1}$$

Where, μ_{ij} is the ith and j^{th} moment for image $f(x, y)$ and given as in Equation (6.2),

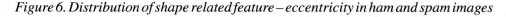

Figure 6. Distribution of shape related feature – eccentricity in ham and spam images

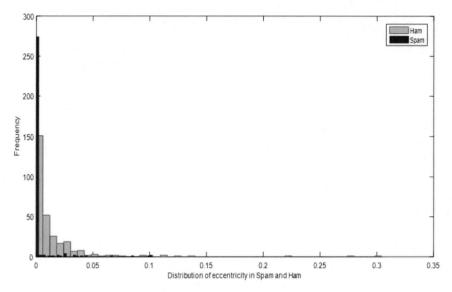

$$\mu_{ij} = \sum_{x}\sum_{y}(x - \bar{x})^{i}(y - \bar{y})^{j}f(x, y) \tag{6.2}$$

Figure 7 shows the distribution of 4th order Zernike moment (absolute value) in both spam and ham images.

All these features extracted are highly dimensional in nature as well as computational intensive; hence the scheme may take more time for further processing. The author also used Tesseract OCR to extract text and classify an image as spam if more than 2 characters found in the image. But OCR based method found to have low accuracy of around 80%; compared to near duplicate and visual feature based methods.

In 2009, the authors proposed FH algorithm which carries out filtering at two levels namely file properties discrimination (such as file size, width, height, and bit depth) in the first and histogram filtering (such as color or gray-level) in the second level (He, Wen and Zheng, 2009). In order to access the similarity among images the file properties were compared to a predefined threshold. If similarity is noticed than classification based on histogram was carried out at second level. The authors claimed the accuracy within the range of 80.60% to 98.50% on various datasets. In the same year, Zuo et al. (2009) used robust Fourier-Mellin Transform (FMT) invariant features as visual features along with one-class classifier, the support vector data description

Figure 7. Distribution of shape related feature – 4th order Zernike moment in ham and spam images

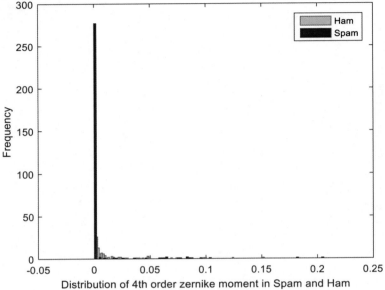

Distribution of 4th order zernike moment in Spam and Ham

(SVDD), for image spam detection. The authors exploit the spam image characteristics like 1) Sending same content many times to the same email account 2) Introducing many variations for a template image spam and 3) Text intensive nature of image spam. Hence; translation, scale and rotation invariant FMT is used which performs well under noise. PCA is applied to FMT matrix and one class SVM is trained with Mark Dredze, SpamArchive and Caltech-256 Dataset. Figure 8 (a) and Figure 8 (b) shows the distribution of Mean of 1st and 2nd Principal Component of Fourier Mellin Transform in Ham and Spam Images respectively. The authors claimed the accuracy of 90% approximately.

Yan et al. (2010) proposed a comprehensive solution for image spam detection that includes both server side cluster analysis and active learning based client side detection. Client side filter extracts 23 image features related to color, texture, shape and appearance domain. The color features include entropy, discreteness, mean, variance, skewness, and kurtosis of color histogram of Red, Green and Blue channels respectively. Figure 9 (a)–(c) shows the distribution of entropy of color histogram of Red, Green and Blue channels respectively both spam images and genuine images. Texture and shape features are calculated using local binary pattern (LBP) and gradient magnitude

Figure 8. Distribution of mean of principal components of Fourier Mellin transform in ham and spam images

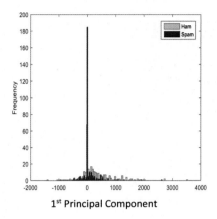

1st Principal Component

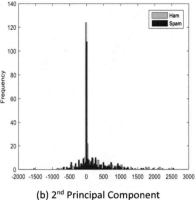

(b) 2nd Principal Component

orientation histogram respectively. Appearance related features are extracted from spatial correlogram of the gray level pixels within 1-neighborhood. Figure 9 (d)-(f) shows the distribution of mean of LBP histogram, number of edges and Geary's index for 1 Neighborhood Spatial Correlogram in both spam images and genuine images respectively.

The authors claimed highest detection accuracy. However; in order to adapt the clustering results with addition of new spam images; server-side cluster analysis need to run in a batch mode on a set of spam images received within a period time. Client side active learning process need to quickly achieve very high true positive rate and maintain extremely low false positive rate at the same time. It will be more annoying for any user to find a misclassified normal image attachment out of the trash box.

In the same year, a three-layer image-spam detection system is proposed by the authors, in their work (Liu, Tsao and Lee, 2010), where first layer analyzes only mail header for fast processing while the second and third layers analyze the high level feature and low level feature of the images that are escaped from first layer. In second layer, selected ten features are width, height, aspect ratio, image format, file size, image area, compression, pixel format, property-id list length and vertical resolution. As low-level feature offers more robust detection but requires high processing time, the escaped images from first two layers are only passed to third layer of detection. However the third layer in this scheme analyzes only color features: color histogram and the color moment for further analysis. Hence, detection accuracy may suffer.

Figure 9. Distribution of features in spam and ham image dataset

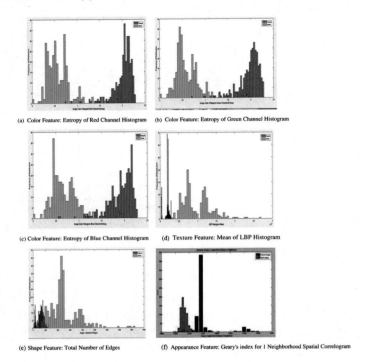

(a) Color Feature: Entropy of Red Channel Histogram   (b) Color Feature: Entropy of Green Channel Histogram

(c) Color Feature: Entropy of Blue Channel Histogram   (d) Texture Feature: Mean of LBP Histogram

(e) Shape Feature: Total Number of Edges   (f) Appearance Feature: Geary's index for 1 Neighborhood Spatial Correlogram

In Chapter 3, figures Figure 2 (a)-(f) shows distribution of first and second order color moments in spam and ham images. The author used both first order and second order moments. Here, first order central moments shows wider separation compared to that of second order central moments here. The threshold for detection is needed to be selected manually for each layer which is tedious task and also affects the generalization of the scheme. The authors claimed the accuracy rate about 94% for their system.

In 2011, Soranamageswari and Meena (2011), used gradient histogram is a key feature for image based spam detection. The extracted features are normalized and then applied as input for feed forward back propagation neural network (BPNN) model. The average classification accuracy stated is around 93.7%, when 90% of the samples are randomly utilized for training and remaining 10% is used for testing in a BPNN. In the same year, Battista Biggio had given a detailed summary of the main characteristics of different image spam detection techniques including OCR based, near duplicate detection based and image feature based image spam detection technique (Biggio et al., 2011). The authors claimed that combination of OCR-based and image classification techniques had increased the detection accuracy through experimental results. Combination of the different kinds of techniques can provide a better discriminant capability between spam and legitimate images.

6.2. ADDITIONAL FEATURES PROPOSED

Following are some additional image features proposed in this book, which can be utilized for image spam detection effectively.

6.2.1. High Level Feature: Exchangeable Image File Format (Exif) Metadata

Exif is a standard that specifies the formats for images/sounds used by digital cameras (Phil, 2016). This standard consists of the Exif image file specification and the Exif audio file specification. The metadata tags defined in the Exif standard includes date/time information, camera related information such as the camera model/make, image capture information such as orientation/rotation, aperture, shutter speed, focal length, along with other descriptions and copyright information. We have used Exiftool.exe tool (Phil, 2016) in order to extract the related metadata information from sample spam and ham images (see Figure 10 (a) and Figure 10 (b) respectively. The output of the tool for both the images is given in Figure 10 (c) and Figure 10 (d) respectively. We can see a lot of difference between the output natural images captured by camera and man generated spam images. The additional attributes related to camera model or make, image capture information or copyright information gives a definite clue about the genuine natural images. Total number of tags or features in natural images is very much higher compared to that of spam images. These metadata can definitely serve as important features in detecting spam images at server end.

6.2.2. Low Level Feature: Noise Estimate

Imaging sensors used in capturing devices tends to introduce various defects and to create noise in the pixel values in these natural images. T (Immerkr, 1996) suggested a fast and simple method for estimating the variance of additive zero mean Gaussian noise in an image. The method provides local estimate of the noise variance across the image using a 3×3 Laplacian mask

Figure 10. Exif data captured using Exiftool

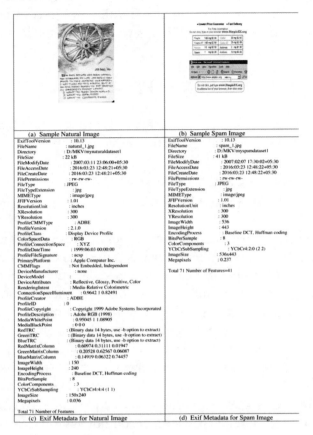

(a) Sample Natural Image	(b) Sample Spam Image
ExifToolVersion : 10.13	ExifToolVersion : 10.13
FileName : natural_1.jpg	FileName : spam_1.jpg
Directory : D:/MKV/mynaturaldataset1	Directory : D:/MKV/myspamdataset1
FileSize : 22 kB	FileSize : 41 kB
FileModifyDate : 2007:03:11 23:06:00+05:30	FileModifyDate : 2007:02:07 17:30:02+05:30
FileAccessDate : 2016:03:23 12:48:21+05:30	FileAccessDate : 2016:03:23 12:48:22+05:30
FileCreateDate : 2016:03:23 12:48:21+05:30	FileCreateDate : 2016:03:23 12:48:22+05:30
FilePermissions : rw-rw-rw-	FilePermissions : rw-rw-rw-
FileType : JPEG	FileType : JPEG
FileTypeExtension : jpg	FileTypeExtension : jpg
MIMEType : image/jpeg	MIMEType : image/jpeg
JFIFVersion : 1.01	JFIFVersion : 1.01
ResolutionUnit : inches	ResolutionUnit : inches
XResolution : 300	XResolution : 300
YResolution : 300	YResolution : 300
ProfileCMMType : ADBE	ImageWidth : 536
ProfileVersion : 2.1.0	ImageHeight : 443
ProfileClass : Display Device Profile	EncodingProcess : Baseline DCT, Huffman coding
ColorSpaceData : RGB	BitsPerSample : 8
ProfileConnectionSpace : XYZ	ColorComponents : 3
ProfileDateTime : 1999:06:03 00:00:00	YCbCrSubSampling : YCbCr4:2:0 (2 2)
ProfileFileSignature : acsp	ImageSize : 536x443
PrimaryPlatform : Apple Computer Inc.	Megapixels : 0.237
CMMFlags : Not Embedded, Independent	
DeviceManufacturer : none	Total 71 Number of Features=41
DeviceModel :	
DeviceAttributes : Reflective, Glossy, Positive, Color	
RenderingIntent : Media-Relative Colorimetric	
ConnectionSpaceIlluminant : 0.9642 1 0.82491	
ProfileCreator : ADBE	
ProfileID : 0	
ProfileCopyright : Copyright 1999 Adobe Systems Incorporated	
ProfileDescription : Adobe RGB (1998)	
MediaWhitePoint : 0.95045 1 1.08905	
MediaBlackPoint : 0 0 0	
RedTRC : (Binary data 14 bytes, use -b option to extract)	
GreenTRC : (Binary data 14 bytes, use -b option to extract)	
BlueTRC : (Binary data 14 bytes, use -b option to extract)	
RedMatrixColumn : 0.60974 0.31111 0.01947	
GreenMatrixColumn : 0.20528 0.62567 0.06087	
BlueMatrixColumn : 0.14919 0.06322 0.74457	
ImageWidth : 150	
ImageHeight : 240	
EncodingProcess : Baseline DCT, Huffman coding	
BitsPerSample : 8	
ColorComponents : 3	
YCbCrSubSampling : YCbCr4:4:4 (1 1)	
ImageSize : 150x240	
Megapixels : 0.036	
Total 71 Number of Features	
(c) Exif Metadata for Natural Image	(d) Exif Metadata for Spam Image

followed by a summation over the image. The method performs well for a large range of noise variance values. The advantage of this method is that it includes a Laplacian operation which is almost insensitive to image structure but only depends on the noise in the image. Figure 11 shows the distribution of noise estimate for both spam and ham images using the method suggested by (Immerkr, 1996).

Thus, the genuine images are likely to have significant noise components. Spam images on the other hand, being computer generated do not get affected from sensor devices/natural light effects and hence; noise features will be different. Spam images are likely to have lesser noise content, unless intentionally introduced by the spammer. Signal-to-noise ratio (SNR) can also be selected as one of the noise related feature. *SNR* is defined as the

Figure 11. Estimated noise in spam and ham images

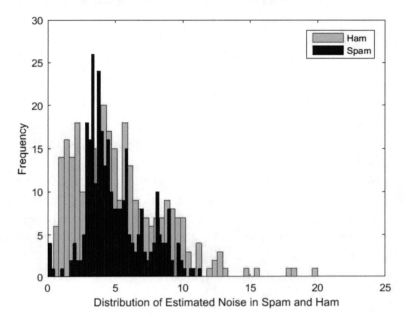

ratio of signal power to the noise power, often expressed in decibels, as in Equation 6.3.

$$SNR_{dB} = 10 \log_{10} \left(\frac{Power_{Signal}}{Power_{Noise}} \right)$$
(6.3)

Where, SNR_{dB} gives the value of Signal to noise ratio in dB, $Power_{Signal}$ is the power of the signal in watts and $Power_{Noise}$ is the power of the noise in watts.

6.2.3. Texture Feature: Using Gabor Wavelet (GW) and Local Phase Quantization (LPQ)

Gabor Wavelet (GW) is extensively used for scrutinizing texture properties and provides optimal resolution in both spatial and frequency domain (Tai, 1996; Isaac et al., 2015, Zhang et al., 2009, Haghighat et al., 2015). It decomposes an image into various multi-scale and multi-orientation sub-bands. GW is

Gaussian kernel modulated by sinusoidal wave. The 2D GW is expressed as in Equation (6.4).

$$\Psi\mu, v(z) = (\|k\mu, v\|^2 / \sigma^2)e - (\|k\mu, v\|^2 z^2 / 2\sigma^2)[e(ik\mu, vZ) - e - (\sigma^2 / 2)] \qquad (6.4)$$

$Z = I(x, y)$, $\|.\|$ = normal operator, v = scale, μ = orientation, $k\mu$, v=wave vector, σ = (Gaussian Window / Standard Deviation of Gaussian window).

For a given 5 scales and 8 orientations, a given input image is decomposed into 40 sub-band images. The number of scales ($1 \leq$ scales ≥ 5) and orientations($1 \leq$ orientations ≥ 8) can be selected as per our requirements and choice. In order to understand better some choices of selected scales and orientations are tabulated below in Table 1.

Sub-band images are achieved by carrying out convolution of input image with the 2D GW as in Equation (6.5).

$$G_{\mu,v}(z) = I(Z) * \Psi_{\mu,v}(z) \qquad (6.5)$$

The scale and orientation of Gabor Filter bank are shown in Figure 12 (a) and Figure 12 (b).

After applying the Gabor filter, Local Phase Quantization (LPQ) is applied to each subband images. LPQ extracts the phase values of every pixel of the subband image by examining the values of its local neighboring pixels. It depends on the blur invariance characteristic of Fourier phase spectrum (Ojansivu and Heikkila, 2008). Image blurring in carried out in order to lower its edge contents so that smooth transition can be achieved from one color to another color. It gives phase information of each sub-band image by

Table 1. No of Sub-bands

Scale (X)	Orientation (Y)	Sub-bands (X ×Y)
1	2	2
2	3	8
3	4	12
4	7	28
5	8	40

Figure 12. Gabor Filter bank

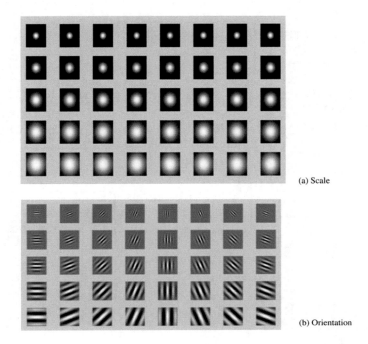

(a) Scale

(b) Orientation

calculating the 2D Short term Fourier Transform around each pixel by taking the rectangular neighborhood. This blur invariant texture information can be used to classify spam images from ham images effectively.

6.3. PROPOSED SCHEME BASED ON GW AND LPQ

Here, we propose a server-client image spam detection model which utilizes the texture feature extracted from GW-LPQ domain along with SVM classifier. The overall architecture of proposed model, server side implementation and client side implementation is as shown in Figure 13, Figure 14 and Figure 15 respectively.

The server side implementation processes GW first sub-band only. This reduces the processing time and computational burden of handling bulk images at server side. The extracted GW-LPQ texture feature is given to SVM classifier for classification. The correctly identified ham images are directly sent to the client email inbox account, correctly detected spam images are

Figure 13. Proposed server-client architecture for image spam detection

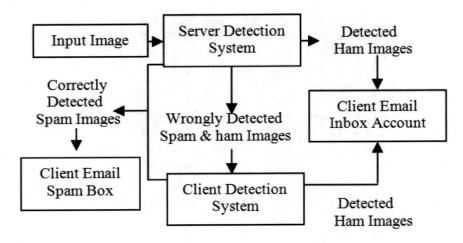

Figure 14. Server side implementation

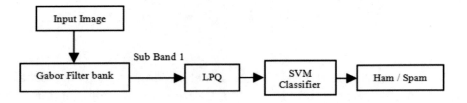

Figure 15. Client side implementation

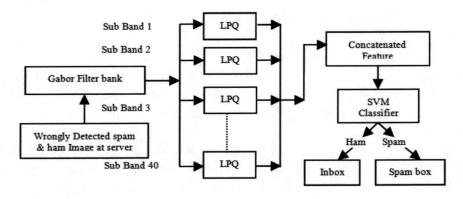

sent to client email spam box account while wrongly detected spam or ham images are again analyzed at the client detection system.

At client side implementation, all 40 sub-bands were selected for processing to achieve maximum accuracy as shown in Figure 15. Selection of 40 sub-bands at client side will not increase much burden as many of the spam images are already segregated by the server detection system. The sub-bands feature are then concatenated and given to SVM classifier for classification. The identified ham images are sent to the client email inbox account and identified spam images are sent to client email spam box.

The experiments are carried out two different available datasets 1) Hunter Dataset (Gao et. al., 2008) containing 928 spam images and 810 ham images in JPEG format 2) Princeton Dataset (Dredze et al., 2007) containing 3299 spam images and 2021 ham images in different formats. Both gray scale and Chrominance (Cr component in YCbCr color space) values of images are used to calculate texture feature.

Experiments were carried out in MATLAB R13. The performance was measured in terms of False positive rate (FPR), True positive rate (TPR), and Accuracy as in Equation (6.6), Equation (6.7) and Equation (6.8) respectively.

$$TPR = (TP/(TP + FN)) \qquad (6.6)$$

$$FPR = (FP/(FP + TN)) \qquad (6.7)$$

$$ACC = 100 \, ((TP + TN)/(TP + TN + FN + FP)) \qquad (6.8)$$

True Positive (TP) = It represent the total number of spam categorized as spam.
False Negative (FN) = It represent the total number of spam categorized as ham.
True Negative (TN) = It represent the total number of ham categorized as ham.
False Positive (FP) = It represent the total number of ham categorized as the spam.
ACC= It reflect the percentage of the correctly specified spam images.

Table 2. Gray Scale Results

Dataset→	Hunter		Princeton	
Results↓	Server	Client	Server	Client
TP	879	44	2769	86
TN	763	19	1636	58
FP	17	1	85	7
FN	24	2	130	9
TPR	0.9734	0.9565	0.9551	0.9052
FPR	0.0217	0.0500	0.0493	0.1076
ACC	97.5638	95.4545	95.3463	90.000

Table 3. Cr Results

Dataset→	Hunter	
Results↓	Server	Client
TP	851	42
TN	733	38
FP	47	4
FN	52	5
TPR	0.9424	0.8936
FPR	0.0602	0.0952
ACC	94.1176	89.8876

The results while considering the gray scale value and Cr value for representing the texture of an image for both the dataset are as tabulated in Table 2 and Table 3. It is clear from the results that gray scale values are better representation of texture of an image as compared to that of Cr value.

For Hunter dataset an accuracy of 97.5638% was achieved at server side and 95.4545% at client side whereas an accuracy of 95.3463% and exactly 90% was achieved at server and client side respectively for Princeton dataset. Cr value experiment was conducted on hunter dataset and an accuracy of 94.1176% at server and 89.8876% at client was achieved.

The results show the strength of proposed texture feature using GW-LPQ to represent low level characteristics for spam images. This scheme exhibits lower processing time along with good detection accuracy.

6.4. COMPARISON OF VARIOUS TECHNIQUES

This section gives the detailed analysis of the works related to image feature based spam detection given in literature. The results are stated in terms of Accuracy, Recall or True Positive Rate, False Positive Rate, Precision and the time required to extract the features in Table 4.

6.5. SUMMARY

This chapter provides the detailed overview of spam detection methods based on different image or visual features. These techniques exploit various properties related to color, shape, texture and noise content along with some high level metadata features. From the distribution of these features, it can be concluded that most of these features have good capability of strongly discriminating spam images from ham images. The chapter also brings out the detailed literature review of existing visual feature based spam detection techniques. The chapter proposes new feature related to metadata, noise and texture domain which can be exploited for spam detection. Further, the chapter proposes a novel server-client image spam detection model based on novel texture feature using GW-LPQ. The strength of image features for image spam detection is proved with the experimental results.

Table 4. Comparison of Visual feature based Image Spam detection techniques

Related Work	Image Features Used	Classifier	Accuracy (%)	Recall/ TPR (%)	FPR (%)	Precision (%)	Time for Feature Extraction (in secs)	Remarks
Krasser, et al., (2007).	Image width, Image height, Aspect ratio, Binary: GIF image, Binary: JPEG image, Binary: PNG image, File size, Image area, Compression	SVM-RBF Kernel resubLoss = 0.1133 TP=61,TN=67,FP=8,FN=14	85.33 =	81.33	10.66	88.40	3.57	Only metadata feature Low computational cost, can be used as first layer of spam detection.
Byungki et al., (2007)	color moments, color heterogeneity, conspicuousness, and self-similarity	MFoM-based learning resubloss=0.055556 TP=66,TN=72,FP=3,FN=9	92.00	88.00	4.00	95.65	30.27	Low level color features, more computational complexity, Multiclass characterization
Gao et al., (2008)	color histogram and gradient histogram features	probabilistic boosting tree resubloss=0.044444 TP=71,TN=69,FP=6,FN=4	93.333333	94.666667	8.000000	92.207792	19.46	Low level color and gradient histogram features, more computational complexity,
Mehta, Nangia and Gupta (2008).	color moments, color coherence, edge freq., autocorrelation, Run length, co-occurance, eccentricity, zernike, legendre features	SVM resubloss=0.055556 TP=72,TN=72,FP=3,FN=3	96.000000	96.000000	4.000000	96.000000	40.24	Color, texture,shape features, High feature dimension, more computational complexity,
Zuo et al.,(2009)	Fourier-Mellin invariant descriptor	One class SVM Classifier resubloss=0.353333 TP=69,TN=31,FP=44,FN=6	66.66	92.00	58.66	61.06	19.53	Low accuracy, high FPR
Gao et al.,(2010)	23 features related to color, texture, shape, appearance	resubloss=0.055556 TP=70,TN=73,FP=2,FN=5	95.33	93.33	2.66	97.22	56.98	Highly dimensional feature, more time complexity, good accuracy, low FPR

continued on next page

Table 4. Continued

Related Work	Image Features Used	Classifier	Accuracy (%)	Recall/ TPR (%)	FPR (%)	Precision (%)	Time for Feature Extraction (in secs)	Remarks
Soranamageswari and C. Meena, (2011)	Image Gradient Features	BPNN classifier resubloss=0.097778 TP=63,TN=74,FP=1,FN=12	91.33	84.00	1.333	98.43	9.40	Low FPR, good feature, medium time complexity
Basheer et al, (2012)	Texture Features: Image histogram, Runlength matrix, Coocurrence matrix, Image gradient, Autoregressive model, Wavelet transform	SVM Classifier resubloss=0.022222 TP=72,TN=73,FP=2,FN=3	96.66	96.00	2.666	97.29	45.40	Only texture features, Highly dimensional feature, more time feature, more time complexity, good accuracy, low FPR
Proposed Scheme using GW-LPQ	Texture Features: Gabor wavelet with local phase quantization	SVM Classifier resubloss=0.033333 TP=74,TN=75,FP=0,FN=1	99.33	98.66	0.000	100.0	158.0	Highest Accuracy, Lowest FPR, More time complexity if analyzed at client side.

143

REFERENCES

Aradhye, H., Myers, G., & Herson, J. A. (2005). Image Analysis for Efficient Categorization of Image-based Spam E-mail. *Proceedings of 8th International Conference on Document Analysis and Recognition (ICDAR-2005)*, 914–918. doi:10.1109/ICDAR.2005.135

Basheer, A., Ismail, K., & Omar, A. (2012). Detecting Image Spam Using Image Texture Features. *International Journal for Information Security Research*, 2(3/4), 344–353.

Biggio, B., Fumera, G., Pillai, I., & Fabio, R. (2011). A Survey and Experimental Evaluation of Image Spam Filtering Techniques. *Pattern Recognition Letters*, 32(10), 1436–1446. doi:10.1016/j.patrec.2011.03.022

Byun, B., Lee, C. H., Webb, S., & Pu, C. (2007). A Discriminative Classifier Learning Approach to Image Modeling and Spam Image Identification. *Proceedings of 4th Conference on Email and Anti-Spam, (CEAS-2007).*

Dredze, M., Gevaryahu, R., & Elias, B. A. (2007). Learning Fast Classifiers for Image Spam. *Proceedings of 4th International Conference on Email and Anti-Spam.*

Gao, Y., Yang, M., Zhao, X., Pardo, B., Wu, Y., Pappas, T. N., & Choudhary, A. N. (2008). Image Spam Hunter. *Proceedings of International Conference on Acoustics, Speech, and Signal Processing (ICASSP-2008),* 1765–1768.

Haghighat, M., Zonouz, S., & Abdel, M. (2015). CloudID: Trustworthy Cloud-based and Cross-enterprise Biometric Identification. *Expert Systems with Applications*, 42(21), 7905–7916. doi:10.1016/j.eswa.2015.06.025

He, P., Wen, X., & Zheng. (2009). A Simple Method for Filtering Image Spam. *Proceedings of 8th IEEE/ACIS International Conference on Computer and Information Science (ICIS-2009)*, 910–913.

Immerkr, J. (1996). *Fast Noise Variance Estimation. Computer Vision and Image Understanding, 64*(2), 300–302. doi:10.1006/cviu.1996.0060

Krasser, S., Yuchun, T., Gould, J., Alperovitch, D., & Judge, P. (2007). Identifying Image Spam Based on Header and File Properties using C4.5 Decision Trees and Support Vector Machine Learning. Proceedings of Information Assurance and Security Workshop (IAW-2007), 255-261.

Lamia, M. K., Munesh, C., & Mohammadi, A. K. (2012). A Study of Image Spam Filtering Techniques. *Proceedings of Fourth International Conference on Computational Intelligence and Communication Networks (CICN-2012)*, 245-250.

Liu, T., Tsao, W., & Lee, C. (2010). A High Performance Image-Spam Filtering System. *Proceedings of Ninth International Symposium on Distributed Computing and Applications to Business, Engineering and Science (DCABES-2010)*, 445-449. doi:10.1109/DCABES.2010.97

Meera, M., & Wilsey, M. (2015). Image Forgery Detection Based on Gabor Wavelets and Local Phase Quantization. *Proceedings of Second International Symposium on Computer Vision and the Internet (VisionNet'15)*, 76-83.

Mehta, B., Nangia, S., Gupta, M., & Nejdl, W. (2008). Detecting Image Spam using Visual Features and Near Duplicate Detection. *Proceedings of 17th International Conference on World Wide Web. (www2008)*, 497–506. doi:10.1145/1367497.1367565

Nhung, N. P., & Phuong, T. M. (2007). An Efficient Method for Filtering Image-Based Spam. *Proceedings of IEEE International Conference on Research, Innovation and Vision for the Future*, 96-102. doi:10.1109/RIVF.2007.369141

Ojansivu, V., & Heikkila, J. (2008). *Blur Insensitive Texture Classification using Local Phase Quantization. In Image and signal processing* (pp. 236–243). Springer.

Phil, H. (2016). *Exiftool By Phil Harvey – Read, Write and Edit Meta Information*. Available from: http://www.sno.phy.queensu.ca/~phil/exiftool/

Soranamageshwari, M., & Meena, C. (2011). A Novel Approach towards Image Spam Classification. *International Journal of Computer Theory and Engineering*, *3*(1), 84–88. doi:10.7763/IJCTE.2011.V3.287

Tahmasbi, A., Saki, F., & Shokouhi, S. B. (2011). Classification of Benign and Malignant Masses Based on Zernike Moments, Journal. *Computers in Biology and Medicine*, *41*(8), 726–735. doi:10.1016/j.compbiomed.2011.06.009 PMID:21722886

Tai, S. L. (1996). Image Representation Using 2D Gabor wavelets. *IEEE Transactions on Pattern Analysis and Machine Intelligence*, *18*(10), 959–971. doi:10.1109/34.541406

Wang, M., Zhang, W., & Zhang, Y. (2011). Detecting Image Spam Based on Cross Entropy. *Proceedings of the Eighth Web Information Systems and Applications Conference (WISA-2011)*, 19-22.

Yan, G., Choudhary, A., & Gang, H. (2010). A Comprehensive Server to Client Side Approach to Image Spam Detection. *IEEE Transactions on Information Forensics and Security*, *5*(4), 826–836. doi:10.1109/TIFS.2010.2080267

Zhang, C., Chen, W., Chen, X., Tiwari, R., Yang, L., & Warner, G. (2009). A Multimodal Data Mining Framework for Revealing Common Sources of Spam Images. *Journal of Multimedia*, *4*(5), 313–320. doi:10.4304/jmm.4.5.313-320

Zuo, H., Li, X., Wu, O., Hu, W., & Luo, G. (2009). Image Spam Filtering using Fourier-mellin Invariant Features. *Proceedings of International Conference on Acoustics, Speech, and Signal Processing (ICASSP-2009)*, 849–852.

Chapter 7
Image Spam Detection Scheme Based on Fuzzy Inference System

ABSTRACT

The evasion techniques used by image spam impose new challenges for e-mail spam filters. Effectual image spam detection requires selection of discriminative image features and suitable classification scheme. Existing research on image spam detection utilizes only visual features such as color, appearance, shape and texture, while no efforts is made to employ statistical noise features. Further, most image spam classification schemes assume existence of clear cut demarcation between extracted features from genuine image and image spam dataset. In this chapter, we attempt to solve these issues; by proposing a novel server side solution called F-ISDS (Fuzzy Inference System based Image Spam Detection Scheme). F-ISDS considers statistical noise features along with the standard image features and meta-data features. F-ISDS employs dimensionality reduction using Principal Component Analysis (PCA) to map selected set of n features into a set of m principal components. Based on the selected significant principal components, input/output membership functions and rules are designed for Fuzzy Inference System (FIS) classifier. FIS provides a computationally simple and an intuitive means of performing the image spam detection. Email server can tag email with this knowledge so that client can take decision as per the local policy. Further, a Linear Regression Analysis is used to model the relationship between selected principal components and extracted features for classification phase. Experimental results confirm the efficacy of the proposed solution.

DOI: 10.4018/978-1-68318-013-5.ch007

7.1. PROBLEM STATEMENT

Since, most e-mail clients render graphics image automatically, image spam can successfully deliver the intended message to the end users. OCR based detection techniques fail when the spammers obfuscate the text in image spam by adding noise, rotating texts etc. The highly unnoticeable changes due to obfuscation techniques used by spammers, result in generation of a huge quantity of image spam containing random patterns with almost no repetitions. The traditional content based or signature based filtering image spam detection techniques tend to fail against such manipulated images.

Most of existing image spam detection techniques either focus on few of the image features which may lead to lesser detection accuracy, or have a high design and computation complexity. Further, it is found that most of the times, a clear cut demarcation between extracted features from genuine image dataset and image spam dataset may not exist. Therefore, there is a need to leverage dominant discriminative image features for effective spam detection etc.

In recent works, fuzzy inference system (FIS) has been successfully employed for object detection and classification applications (Nelson, 2001, Inan and Elif, 2004, Nazmy et al., 2005). However, the use of FIS has not been explored for spam detection applications. FIS technique offers a computationally efficient, intuitive and robust means of classification. This technique can further accommodate the expert input as well (Nelson, 2001).

To deal with mentioned problems, this work proposes a unique server side solution called F-ISDS (Fuzzy Inference System based Image Spam Detection Scheme) for mitigation of image spam e-mails. Proposed F-ISDS suggests use of statistical noise features along with the color, appearance, shape, texture and metadata related features. To reduce design complexity, Principal Component Analysis (PCA) is employed to map selected set of n features into a set of m principal components. Since, most of the extracted features do not have a clear cut threshold for differentiating between spam and genuine dataset and there is a blurred differentiation between the two, leading to fuzzy classes.

Hence, a Fuzzy Inference System (FIS) is designed for image spam detection and classification. FIS provides a computationally simple means of performing the classification functions and the proposed F-ISDS can easily be expanded for utilizing other feature inputs. To the best of our knowledge, this is the first work suggesting use of FIS for Image Spam Detection.

7.2. PROPOSED F-ISDS

The proposed model consists of Feature Extraction Module, PCA Module, Linear Regression Analysis Module and FIS based classifier as shown in Figure 1.

Given a batch of image attachments from an e-mail server, the Feature Extraction Module would first extract significant features from each image. During the training phase, the selected set of n features, F_n are mapped onto a set of m principal components C_m, using PCA module. Linear Regression Analysis is used to model the relationship between C_m and F_n. Based on the selected significant C_m values, input/output membership functions and rules are designed for Fuzzy Inference System (FIS) based classifier. In classification

Figure 1. Proposed F-ISDS model

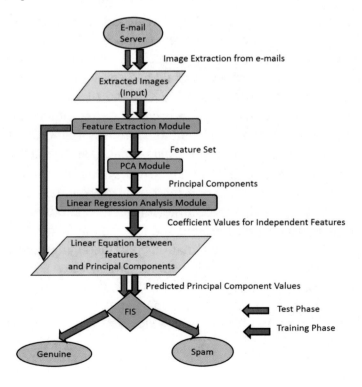

phase, the features $\hat{F}_n$ are extracted from the test image dataset and are used to predict the principal components $\hat{C}_m$, using the linear equations modeled during the training phase. The $\hat{C}_m$ values are then fed to the designed FIS and used to classify into Genuine (Ham) or Spam.

7.2.1. Feature Extraction Module

Various features differentiating the spam images from genuine images are extracted from different domains like metadata (Zin and Nyein, 2014)), color, shape, texture, appearance and spatial information (Gao et al., 2008) for a standard dataset consisting both spam images and genuine images. The effects of noise content are also analysed for spam detection using statistical noise features like Entropy of Noise and Signal to noise ratio (SNR). After rigorous simulation and empirical analysis, total seven significant features are selected for further analysis. The description of these 7 features is given below:

Genuine image, as captured by any image capturing device like a camera, is likely to have more information contained in the colors. These genuine images are likely to have more number of colors and shades. Whereas, spam images being primarily computer generated are generally composed of fewer number of colors and shades, as the general purpose of the spammer is to convey the intended information to the recipient by means of eye-catching color composition. During experimental analysis, it is found that the color features - entropy of color histogram (F_1, F_2, F_3) of Red, Green and Blue channels respectively contributes more compared to other color features stated in G. Yan et al. (2010) for differentiating images. Figure 2 (a)–(c) shows the distribution of (F_1, F_2, F_3) for both spam images and genuine images.

The local binary pattern (LBP) contained in the image reveals the similarity or differences between the neighbouring pixels and can be used to analyse texture information. Since, the genuine images are captured in a natural environment with varying background and foreground features, the genuine images are likely to have more information contained in the LBP histogram. Spam images on the other hand, being computer generated are likely to have smoother background and foreground features, and thus likely to contain less information in the LBP histogram. During simulation, it is found that the mean of LBP histogram (F_4) serves as a significant texture related feature (see Figure 2 (d)).

Figure 2. Distribution of Features in Spam and Ham Image Dataset (Gao et al., 2016)

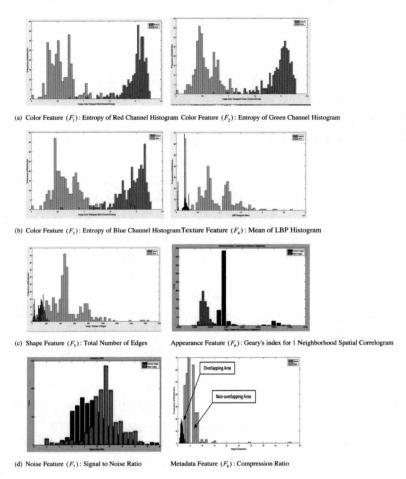

(a) Color Feature (F_1): Entropy of Red Channel Histogram   Color Feature (F_2): Entropy of Green Channel Histogram

(b) Color Feature (F_3): Entropy of Blue Channel Histogram   Texture Feature (F_4): Mean of LBP Histogram

(c) Shape Feature (F_5): Total Number of Edges   Appearance Feature (F_6): Geary's index for 1 Neighborhood Spatial Correlogram

(d) Noise Feature (F_7): Signal to Noise Ratio   Metadata Feature (F_8): Compression Ratio

As the spam images are generally a combination of text and images, they are likely to have more textual information. Thus, spam images are likely to have more number of edges compared to genuine images. The total amount of edges (F_5) in the image serves as a significant shape related feature (Gao et al., 2010). The distribution of F_5 for genuine and spam images is given in Figure 2 (e).

A spatial correlogram of the gray level pixels, is extracted to get appearance related feature called Geary's spatial index, which is given by Equation 7.1.

$$c(d) = \frac{\frac{1}{2W}\sum_{h=1}^{n}\sum_{i=1}^{n} w_{hi}(y_h - y_i)^2}{\frac{1}{(n-1)}\sum_{i=1}^{n}(y_i - \bar{y})^2}, \text{for} \quad h \neq i \tag{7.1}$$

where, y_h and y_i are the values of the observed variable at sites h and i. The weights take the value $w_{hi} = 1$ when sites h and i are at distance d and $w_{hi} = 0$, otherwise. W is the sum of the weights w_{hi} for the given distance class. For a given distance class, the weights w_{hi} are written in a $(n \times n)$ matrix W. Gearys spatial index $c(d)$ is used as an appearance related feature, F_6. Strong autocorrelation produces low values of $c(d)$. Positive autocorrelation translates in values of $c(d)$ between 0 and 1, whereas, negative autocorrelation produces values larger than 1. The distribution of $c(d)$ for genuine and spam images is given in Figure 2 (f). The spam images are artificially generated and thus are expected to have strong autocorrelation with neighboring pixels, and thus lower positive value of c. However, on the other hand, genuine images generally would have lower positive auto-correlation with the neighbors as these are likely to be in a continuously varying background, and hence have higher positive value of Geary's coefficient c.

The noise content in a given image can convey valuable information about the class of image. The genuine images are generally captured by means of any image-capturing device like a camera and hence, are subject to various kinds of noise due to the ISO settings, exposure time, jitter, electronic noise, etc. Thus, the genuine images are likely to have significant noise components. Spam images on the other hand, being computer generated do not get affected from sensor devices/natural light effects and hence; noise features will be different. Spam images are likely to have lesser noise content, unless intentionally introduced by the spammer. In the proposed system, Signal-to-noise ratio (SNR) as given in Equation 7.2 is selected as noise related feature F_7. SNR is defined as the ratio of signal power to the noise power, often expressed in decibels, as in Equation 2.

$$SNR_{dB} = 10\log_{10}\left(\frac{Power_{Signal}}{Power_{Noise}}\right) \tag{7.2}$$

Where, SNR_{dB} gives the value of Signal to noise ratio in dB, $Power_{Signal}$ is the power of the signal in watts and $Power_{Noise}$ is the power of the noise in watts. The distribution of SNR for genuine and spam images is given in Figure 2 (g).

Besides visual features, content independent meta-data descriptors also found effective for spam detection. The file meta-data gives the information about the file size, dimensions, file format, time of creation/ modification, etc. The compression ratio (Zin and Nyein, 2014) is calculated from a meta-data information as in Equation 7.3.

$$Compression\_Ratio = \frac{filewidth \times fileheight \times bitdepth}{filesize} \qquad (7.3)$$

Spammers would prefer to achieve a higher compression ratio, as they would like the spam images to be small in size and easily deliverable. It is thus expected that spam images will have higher compression ratio as compared to genuine images. Thus, compression ratio has been retained as significant feature F_8 extracted from meta-data. Figure 2 (h) provides the distribution of compression ratio for both genuine and spam images.

Thus for spam classification, a final feature set $F = (F_1,..., F_8)$ containing selected unique and significant features is constructed during initial stage of analysis.

7.2.2. PCA Module

To reduce both computation and design complexity, Principal Component Analysis (PCA) is employed to convert selected set of n features, F_n into a set of m principal components, C_m. PCA technique is used for dimension reduction to identify underlying variables/factors, which explain the pattern of correlations within a set of observed variables. Factor analysis is used in data reduction to identify a small number of factors that explain most of the variance that is observed in a much larger number of manifest variables.

Principal component analysis (PCA) is a statistical procedure that uses an orthogonal transformation to convert a set of observations of possibly correlated variables into a set of values of linearly uncorrelated variables called principal components. The number of principal components is less than or equal to the number of original variables. This transformation is defined in such a way that the first principal component has the largest possible variance (that is, accounts for as much of the variability in the data as possible), and each succeeding component in turn has the highest variance possible under the constraint that it is orthogonal to the preceding components. In short, PCA reduces dimensionality of data is reduced while minimizing the loss of information or distortion.

For dimension reduction using PCA, IBM SPSS Statistics 22 version is used. A suitable Eigen value threshold τ is selected to generate Principal component set $C = \{C_j \,\|\, 1 \le j \le m\}$ from the given input feature set F, which is capable of capturing all selected unique features from F. Thus, a final reduced component set $C = \{C_j \,\|\, 1 \le j \le m\}$ containing selected unique components will act as input for FIS design module. This stage reduces the design complexity of FIS module significantly. In our case, we have selected τ such that, $m = 3$ i.e. top 3 PCA components with high variance will be selected. The distribution for generated sample component, C in both genuine and spam images is as given in Figure 3 respectively.

7.2.3. Linear Regression Analysis Module

A Linear Regression Analysis Module is used to model the relationship between scalar dependent variable C_m and independent variable F_n for classification phase. In linear regression, data are modeled using linear

Figure 3. Distribution for Sample Component C1

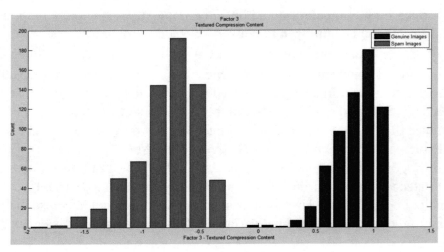

predictor functions, and unknown model parameters are estimated from the data. If the goal is prediction, or forecasting, or reduction, linear regression can be used to fit a predictive model to an observed data set of y and x values. After developing such a model, if an additional value of x is then given without its accompanying value of y, the fitted model can be used to make a prediction of the value of y. Linear Regression analysis helps to identify the values of coefficients $A, B, ..., N$ for the independent variables $F_1, F_2, ..., F_n$ and a constant z, to give a linear equation between dependent variable C and $F_1, F_2, ..., F_n$ as given in Equation 7.4.

$$C = AF_1 + BF_2 + ... + NF_n + z \tag{7.4}$$

During classification/testing stage, the calculated coefficient values $A, B, ..., N$ and z for $\hat{F}$ will be used, to predict $\hat{C}$.

7.2.4. Fuzzy Inference System Design

Traditional classification techniques based on Maximum Entropy (MaxEnt), Naive Bayes (NB), ID3 Decision Tree (DT), SVM, Bayesian Network (BN), and Random Forest (RF) generally focus on text based spam images. However, with the emergence of newer techniques, the spam images have become much similar to genuine images in a number of aspects. These images are likely to lead to confusion for these classifiers, as there is no clear-cut threshold value differentiating the two. To deal with these problems, we propose the use of a Fuzzy inference system based classification model. The fuzzy theory suggests that features be linguistically valued, e.g., the feature size can have values like low, high, etc.

In our approach, we propose using a Sugeno fuzzy model for image classification, which is the heart of our proposed F-ISDS. The simulation results for C_1, C_2 and C_3 are given in Table 1.

Based on the simulation results, each of the input component is fuzzified and divided into 2 linguistic classes - Low and High. The FIS model is designed to have two class output Genuine and Spam. In our model, trapezoidal membership functions have been used. It is found that when a component value becomes greater than/less than a certain value, there is no additional benefit/detriment achieved for properly classifying potential spam. A brief description of each of the inputs and the output and their associated membership functions follows. Figure 6 shows the input components membership functions.

Table 1. Simulation results for Component Set

Feature	Spam Images				Genuine Images				Selected Cross-Over Point
	Mean	Min	Max	Standard Deviation	Mean	Min	Max	Standard Deviation	
C_1	0.3384	-2.8063	6.0844	0.9018	-0.3593	-2.2119	3.1871	0.9383	0
C_2	-0.6216	-3.3163	1.2755	0.6475	0.7292	-7.4225	2.5080	0.6218	0.35
C_3	-0.7819	-3.1751	-0.2673	0.2876	0.8434	-1.2828	1.1403	0.2079	0.2

The input C_1 uses two membership functions: Low (L) and High (H). Table 1 shows that 0 (zero) can be selected as the cross-over point between low and high. The component value greater than 0 (zero), indicates more belongingness to the spam images, and genuine otherwise. There is an overlap of values for approximately 30 percent between spam and genuine images in C_1. Typically, in case of fuzzy inference systems, the overlap of membership functions for any input feature/component is set empirically. Both C_2 and C_3 components use two membership functions: Low (L) and High (H). The values of C_2 below 0.35 indicate likely spam images (targets). The values of C_3 below 0.2 indicate likely spam images (targets). There is almost no overlap for these two component values, making these two more significant in classification.

The corresponding membership functions for these components are as given in Figure 3, Figure 4 and Figure 5 respectively.

A description of the rules used for designing FIS is given in the Algorithm 1.

Figure 4. C_1 Membership Function

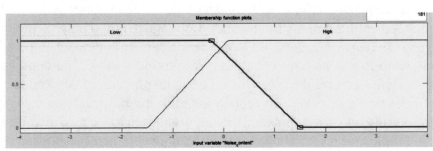

Figure 5. C_2 Membership Function

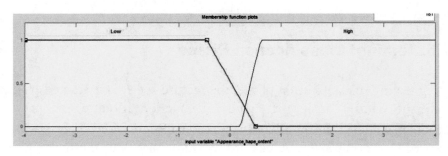

Figure 6. C_3 Membership Function

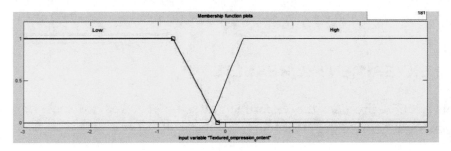

Algorithm 1 Rules for FIS Design
Input: *Fuzzy Components* C_1, C_2, C_3
Output: Output Fuzzy Class – Genuine or Spam
If ($C_2 = High$) AND ($C_3 = High$) then
$\qquad$ (Output Class=Genuine)
End if
If ($C_2 = Low$) AND ($C_3 = Low$) then
$\qquad$ (Output Class=Spam)
End if
If ($C_2 \neq C_3$) then
If ($C_1 = Low$) then (Output Class=Genuine)
Else (Output Class=Spam)
End if
End if

The membership functions and rules were developed primarily by analyzing component values generated from data sets.

7.2.5. Testing/ Classification Phase

During testing/ classification phase, the feature set $\hat{F}$ is extracted from the test image dataset using the Feature Extraction Module and principle component values, $\hat{C}$ are predicted using Linear Regression Analysis Module. The predicted component values are fed in as inputs to the designed FIS, leading to the output as Genuine or Spam class. The server side solution is based on these classification results, as well as, the policies designed at server. As per the policy, if the spam is to be forwarded to the client, then it may be marked as spam and forwarded, else can be dropped at the server itself.

7.3. EXPERIMENTAL RESULTS

This section presents the experimental setup required for the empirical evaluation along with performance comparison.

7.3.1. Dataset

Unlike general image classification task, very few standard image spam corpora are public available due to privacy concerns. In order to gain better and insightful results for performance comparison, we select two datasets for the empirical study.

Dataset 1

Image Spam Hunter dataset is one which is publicly available on the Northwestern University website (Image Spam Hunter Dataset, 2016). The dataset consists of a total of 928 spam images and 810 genuine images (including 20 scanned documents). The same dataset has been earlier used by Gao et al., (2008). The dataset consists of images in.bmp, .jpeg, and .png formats. The available dataset 1 has been divided into two parts training data set 1consisting of 638 genuine images and 680 spam images and test data set 1 consisting of 159 genuine and 229 spam images. The dataset 1 has been used for training of our model.

Dataset 2

It is a real-time dataset consisting of 400 images (200 spam and genuine images each). All the spam images have been collected from 25different personal e-mail accounts held with three popular online web-based e-mail service providers Gmail, Rediff, and Yahoo. As the spammers have been keeping up pace with ways and means to bypass the spam filters, this helps us evaluate the efficacy of our model on the current image dataset. This dataset has been included for testing phase only.

7.3.2. Feature Set Extraction

The details of parameters used for extracting image feature set $\hat{F}$ using Feature extraction module are discussed as:

To calculate F_1, F_2, F_3, a 103 dimension color histogram is built in the RGB space by quantizing each color band into 10 different levels (Gao et al., 2010). For feature F_4, a 59-dimensional texture histogram is extracted, including 58 bins for all the different uniform local binary patterns, i.e., the pattern of at most two 0-1 transitions in an 8-bit stream, and an additional bin for all other non-uniform local binary patterns to calculate entropy of LBP histogram (Gao et al., 2010). For extracting the feature F_5, canny edge detector has been used. For feature F_6, $c(d)$ as given in Equation (1) above, is calculated for distance $D = [D_{hi}] = 1$. Thus, weight $w_{hi} = 1$, for all distances, $D = 1$ and $w_{hi} = 0$ otherwise. To extract noise based features, F_7, we have used a Wiener filter - an adaptive filter based on a statistical approach, used to produce an estimate of a desired or target random process by linear time invariant filtering of an observed noisy process. For calculating F_8, we have extract the file meta-data information from the image. The feature extraction has been carried out using MATLAB R2013a version. The extracted feature set acts as input to the next stage.

7.3.3. PCA Module

For dimension reduction using PCA, IBM SPSS Statistics 22 version is used. A suitable Eigen value threshold of 0.9 is selected to generate Principal component set C from the given input feature set F, which is capable of capturing all the relevant unique features from F. The components

$C_1, C_2 and C_3$ be retained and used for further analysis. The high value of the features indicate a higher correlation of these with the components.

7.3.4. Linear Regression Analysis Module

We carry out Linear Regression Analysis using IBM SPSS Statistics 22, with each of these components as dependent variables and underlying features as independent variables to arrive at a linear equation. Linear regression analysis provides us with the components of the independent variables and a constant by optimization and best fit approach. This method gives an approximate predictive value, given the values of independent features. Linear equations for each component (refer Equation 4) are generated based on the training data set 1 using IBM SPSS Statistics tool.

7.3.5. Fuzzy Inference System

Sugeno method of classification has been employed here, in order to take advantage of the speed and training capabilities associated with this style of inference system. The target con_dence system output uses two membership functions: Genuine and Spam. For the AND operation product (*prod*) and for OR operation probabilistic OR (*probor*) method has been employed. The *probor* is given by Equation 7.4.

$$probor(a,b) = a + b - a \times b \qquad (7.4)$$

The membership functions and rules are developed primarily by analyzing the results obtained from the standard training dataset1. All of the rules are executed with AND operations. Every rule has been given equal weightage of 1 and minimum (min) method has been applied for Implication process to arrive at the fuzzy set. After proper weighting has been assigned to each rule, the implication method is implemented, which weights appropriately the linguistic characteristics that are attributed to it. The aggregate of a fuzzy set encompasses a range of output values, and so must be defuzzified in order to resolve a single output value from the set. Maximum (max) method has been employed for aggregation process in our model. For defuzzification we use the weighted average (*wtavg*) method to arrive at a final crisp value as the output.

7.3.6. Evaluation

The proposed F-ISDS is evaluated based on accuracy, precision and recall. Accuracy is the proportion of true results (both true positives and true negatives) among the total number of cases examined and is as given in Equation 7.5.

$$Accuracy = \frac{TruePositive + TrueNegative}{TruePositive + TrueNegative + FalsePositive + FalseNegative}$$

$$(7.5)$$

Precision (also called positive predictive value) is the fraction of retrieved instances that are relevant, while recall (also known as sensitivity) is the fraction of relevant instances that are retrieved. In a classification problem, the precision for a class is the number of true positives (i.e. the number of items correctly labeled as belonging to the positive class) divided by the total number of elements labeled as belonging to the positive class (i.e. the sum of true positives and false positives, which are items incorrectly labeled as belonging to the class) and is as given in Equation 7.6.

$$\Pr ecision = \frac{TruePositive}{TruePositive + FalsePositive} \qquad (7.6)$$

Recall in this context is defined as the number of true positives divided by the total number of elements that actually belong to the positive class (i.e. the sum of true positives and false negatives, which are items which were not labeled as belonging to the positive class but should have been) and is as given in Equation 7.7.

$$\operatorname{Re} call = \frac{TruePositive}{TruePositive + FalseNegative} \qquad (7.7)$$

To further assess the efficacy of the model, we have used 5-fold cross validation. Cross-validation is a model validation technique for assessing how the results of statistical analysis will generalize to an independent data set. The goal of cross validation is to define a dataset to "test" the model in the training phase (i.e., the validation dataset), in order to limit problems like over fitting, give an insight on how the model will generalize to an independent dataset (i.e., an unknown dataset, for instance from a real problem), etc. One round of cross-validation involves partitioning a sample of data into complementary subsets, performing the analysis on one subset (called the training set), and validating the analysis on the other subset (called the validation set or testing set). To reduce variability, multiple rounds of cross-validation are performed using different partitions, and the validation results are averaged over the 19 rounds.

In our analysis we have use 80% training and 20% test dataset. In 5-fold cross-validation, the original sample is randomly partitioned into 5 equal size subsamples. Of the 5 subsamples, a single subsample is retained as the validation data for testing the model, and the remaining 4 subsamples are used as training data. The cross-validation process is then repeated 5 times (the folds), with each of the 5 subsamples used exactly once as the validation data. The results obtained from the 5 folds are then averaged to produce a single estimation. The Accuracy, Precision and recall for the Training dataset 1 are as given in Table 2.

The Accuracy, Precision and recall for the Test dataset 1 are as given in Table 3.

The results obtained show that test data is following the trends for the training data, showing that the model is not an over-fit. In order to check how the developed model, will adapt to an independent dataset, we also used 5 fold cross-validation and found that the average training accuracy and testing accuracy of 0.9441 and 0.9440 respectively. The average value for Accuracy, Precision and Recall for test dataset and training dataset are almost same thus, showing that the classifier model developed can be generalized to any independent dataset.

Table 2. Evaluation results of training dataset 1

Accuracy	0.9445
Precision	0.9220
Recall	0.9694

Table 3. Evaluation results of test dataset 1

Accuracy	0.9402
Precision	0.9345
Recall	0.9199

To further combine the evaluation parameters, we calculate the F-score, which is the harmonic mean of Precision and Recall. The F-score (Equation 7.8) gives us the relation between data positive labels and those given by the classifier.

$$F - score = \frac{2 \times \mathrm{Pr}\,ecision \times \mathrm{Re}\,call}{\mathrm{Pr}\,ecision + \mathrm{Re}\,call} \tag{7.8}$$

The F-score obtained for both training and test data is 0.8532. Finally, the model developed is tested for its efficacy against the real time images collected and forming a part of the dataset 2. The results obtained are given in the Table 4.

The Fuzzy based classifier has not been used in the field of image spam detection earlier. Since the dataset1 has been used by Gao et al. (2008), the results obtained can be compared with their results. On comparison, it reveals that the approach adopted by Image Spam hunter led to 89.44% detection rate of spam at FP rate 0.86%. However, our method when tested on the real dataset, Dataset2, gives us a classification accuracy of 95.25% with False Positive Rate as 0. This is desirous as we do not want a genuine image to be misclassified as spam, as it would lead to increase in the work load of the user to actually dig through spam e-mails to extract these misclassified genuine images. Thus, proposed F-ISDS outperforms when False Positive rate is considered along with accuracy.

7.4. CONCLUSION

The proposed server side solution F-ISDS demonstrates the application of Fuzzy Inference System for effective image spam detection. To increase the accuracy of detection, statistical noise features are considered along with the color, appearance, shape, texture and metadata related features. Experimental results show the significance of selected noise features for effective image spam

Table 4. Evaluation results of dataset 2

Accuracy	0.9525
Precision	0.9050
Recall	1.0000

163

classification. Further to reduce the design and computational complexity of overall system, F-ISDS utilizes different strategies like construction of limited significant feature set, extraction of components from feature set, selection of significant components for designing FIS; and employing LRA to generate simple linear equations for mapping features to components. Designed FIS is found effective in dealing with the features that do not have clear cut demarcation between genuine and spam. Besides being computationally simpler, FIS needs one time design effort. Experimental results confirm the efficacy of the proposed solution with zero False Positive Rate. The accuracy of detection may be enhanced in future either by integrating IP tracing techniques and/or investigating more discriminative spam image features.

REFERENCES

W3TECHS. (2014). *Usage of Image File Formats for Websites*. Available from: https://w3techs.com/technologies/overview/image_format/all

Apache Spam Assassin. (2009). *Welcome to SpamAssassin*. Available from: http://wiki.apache.org/spamassassin/

Basheer, A., Ismail, K., & Omar, A. (2011). Texture Analysis-Based Image Spam Filtering. *Proceedings of6th International Conference on Internet Technology and Secured Transactions*, 288-293.

COMMTOUCH. (2013). *Internet Threats Trends Report –October 2013*. Available from: http://www.commtouch.com/uploads/pdf/Commtouch-Internet-Threats-Trend-Report-Q3-2013.pdf

Dredze, M., Gevaryahu, R., & Elias, B. A. (2007). Learning Fast Classifiers for Image Spam. *Proceedings of 4th International Conference on Email and Anti-Spam*.

Gao, Y., Yang, M., & Zhao, X. (2016). *Image Spam Hunter Dataset*. Available from: http://www.cs.northwestern.edu/~yga751/ML/ISH.htm#dataset

Gao, Y., Yang, M., Zhao, X., Pardo, B., Wu, Y., Pappas, T. N., & Choudhary, A. N. (2008). Image Spam Hunter. *Proceedings of International Conference on Acoustics, Speech, and Signal Processing (ICASSP-2008)*, 1765–1768.

Hou, Y., Zhao, B., Zhang, H., & Yan, H. (2012). A Fast image spam filter based on ORB. *Proceedings of 3rd IEEE International Conference on Network Infrastructure and Digital Content (IC-NIDC 2012)*, 503-507. doi:10.1109/ICNIDC.2012.6418804

Inan, G., & Elif, D. U. (2004). Application of Adaptive Neuro-fuzzy Inference System for Detection of Electrocardiographic Changes in Patients with Partial Epilepsy using Feature Extraction. *Expert Systems with Applications*, *27*(3), 323–330. doi:10.1016/j.eswa.2004.05.001

Jialie, S., Robert, H. D., Zhiyong, C., Liqiang, N., & Yan, S. (2015). On Robust Image Spam Filtering via Comprehensive Visual Modeling. *Journal of Pattern Recognition, Elsevier*, *48*(10), 3227–3238. doi:10.1016/j.patcog.2015.02.027

MAAWG Organization. (2011). *Email Metrics Program: The Network Operators' Perspective*. Available from: https://www.m3aawg.org/sites/default/files/document/MAAWG_2011_Q1-4_Metrics_Report15Rev.pdf

Nazmy, T. M., El-Messiry, H., & Al-Bokhity, B. (2010). Adaptive Neuro-fuzzy Inference System for Classification of ECG Signals. *Journal of Theoretical and Applied Information Technology*, *12*(2), 71–76.

Nelson, B. N. (2001). Automatic Vehicle Detection in Infrared Imagery Using a Fuzzy Inference-Based Classification System. *IEEE Transactions on Fuzzy Systems*, *9*(1), 53–61. doi:10.1109/91.917114

Pal, S. K., & Dwijesh, K. D. M. (1986). *Fuzzy Mathematical Approach to Pattern Recognition*. Halsted Press New York.

Symantec. (2014). *Symantec Report*. Available from: http://www.symantec.com/securityresponse/landing/spam/

Yan, G., Choudhary, A., & Gang, H. (2010). A Comprehensive Server to Client Side Approach to Image Spam Detection. *IEEE Transactions on Information Forensics and Security*, *5*(4), 826–836. doi:10.1109/TIFS.2010.2080267

Zin, M. W., & Nyein, A. (2014). Detecting Image Spam Based on File Properties, Histogram and Hough Transform. *Journal of Advances in Computer Networks*, *2*(4), 287–292. doi:10.7763/JACN.2014.V2.127

Appendix

A. COMPILATION OF CODE SNIPPETS

A.1. Code to Prepare Dataset

This code reads the images downloaded from image spam hunter dataset and strores them with proper naming convention like if original ham image in the directory has name say 'abc.jpg' then it will be saved as 'Natural001.jpg'. Similarly, if it is a spam image then saved as 'Spam001.jpg'.

```
clc;
clear all;
close all;
```

   % create dataset for training and testing containing 300 natural and 300 spam images from hunter dataset

```
f1 = fullfile('D:/MKV/NaturalImages/NaturalImages', '*.jpg');
totalfiles1=dir(f1);
f2 = fullfile('D:/MKV/SpamImages/SpamImages', '*.jpg');
totalfiles2=dir(f2);
for i=1:300

    filename1=totalfiles1(i).name;
    str = strcat('D:/MKV/NaturalImages/
NaturalImages/',filename1);
    str1 = sprintf('D:/MKV/mynaturaltestdataset1/natural_%d.
jpg',i-500);
    copyfile(str,str1);

    filename2=totalfiles2(i).name;
    str = strcat('D:/MKV/SpamImages/SpamImages/',filename2);
    str2 = sprintf('D:/MKV/myspamtestdataset1/spam_%d.
jpg',i-500);
```

```
    copyfile(str,str2);

end
```

A.2. Read Dataset

This code reads the prepared dataset containing all 300 ham and spam images for further processing.

```
function [ data1,data2 ] = Read_dataset(numrows,numcols)

naturalimgPath = 'D:/MKV/mynaturaldataset1/';
dCell1 = dir([naturalimgPath '*.jpg']);
spamimgPath = 'D:/MKV/myspamdataset1/';
dCell2 = dir([spamimgPath '*.jpg']);

% create an empty cell array
SpamImgSeq={};
NaturalImgSeq={};

disp('Loading natural and spam image files...');

for d = 1:length(dCell2)
a1=imread([spamimgPath dCell2(d).name]);
a1=imresize(a1, [numrows numcols]);
SpamImgSeq{d} = a1;
a2=imread([naturalimgPath dCell1(d).name]);
a2=imresize(a2, [numrows numcols]);
NaturalImgSeq{d}= a2;
end

data1=NaturalImgSeq;
data2=SpamImgSeq;

end
```

A.3. Main Program

```
clc;
clear all;
close all;
% read natural image and spam image dataset for preprocessing
 naturalimgPath = 'D:/MKV/mynaturaldataset1/';
```

```
dCell1 = dir([naturalimgPath '*.jpg']);
spamimgPath = 'D:/MKV/myspamdataset1/';
dCell2 = dir([spamimgPath '*.jpg']);
NaturalImgSeq = {};    % create an empty cell array
SpamImgSeq={};
disp('Loading natural and spam image files...');
for d = 1:length(dCell1)
NaturalImgSeq{d} = imread([naturalimgPath dCell1(d).name]);
SpamImgSeq{d} = imread([spamimgPath dCell2(d).name]);
end
% Define the number of arrays depending upon the number of
features % %required to be extracted
% for e.g. NFeature1 holds feature 1 of ham image features and
SFeature % holds feature 1 of Spam image features
%here we have shown some sample image feature extraction like
image file size, image area, compression factor, aspect ratio,
NFeature1=[];
SFeature1=[];
NFeature2=[];
SFeature2=[];
NFeature3=[];
SFeature3=[];
NFeature4=[];
SFeature4=[];
NFeature5=[];
SFeature5=[];
NFeature6=[];
SFeature6=[];
NFeature7=[];
SFeature7=[];

[ data1,data2 ] = Read_dataset(150,150);
ntotal=300;
% to get elapsed CPU time in secs
starttime = cputime;

for i = 1:ntotal

 % extract meta data features

 info1=imfinfo([naturalimgPath dCell1(d).name]);
 info2=imfinfo([spamimgPath dCell2(d).name]);

 % get File Size
 NFeature1=[NFeature1 info1.FileSize];
 SFeature1=[SFeature1 info2.FileSize];

% calculate Image Area
 temp1=info1.Width*info1.Height;
```

```
 temp2=info2.Width*info2.Height;
 NFeature2=[NFeature2 temp1];
 SFeature2=[SFeature2 temp2];
% calculate Compression Factor
 temp3=temp1/info1.FileSize;
 temp4=temp2/info2.FileSize;
 NFeature3=[NFeature3 temp3];
 SFeature3=[SFeature3 temp4];

% calculate Aspect Ratio
  NFeature4=[NFeature4 info1.Width/info1.Height];
  SFeature4=[SFeature4 info2.Width/info2.Height;];

    x1=data1{i};
    x2=data2{i};
   %calculate color saturation feature

    if(size(x1,3)==3)
    gx1 = rgb2gray(x1);
    [colsat1] = colorSaturation(x1);
    else gx1=x1;
    end

    if(size(x2,3)==3)
    gx2 = rgb2gray(x2);
    [colsat2] = colorSaturation(x2);
    else gx2=x2;
    end

    SizeX1 = size(gx1, 1);
    SizeY1 = size(gx1, 2);

    SizeX2 = size(gx2, 1);
    SizeY2 = size(gx2, 2);

    NFeature5=[NFeature5 colsat1];
    SFeature5=[SFeature5 colsat2];

    [ wcoeff1 ] = fouriermellin(gx1);
    NFeature6=[NFeature6 mean(wcoeff1(:,1))];

    [ wcoeff2 ] = fouriermellin(gx2);
    SFeature6=[SFeature6 mean(wcoeff2(:,1))];

%compute as many as feature required, by defining
getfeature_x() function %for each feature

end
```

```
% normalize features
maxnf1=max(NFeature1(:));
NFeature1=NFeature1./maxnf1;
maxnf2=max(NFeature2(:));
NFeature2=NFeature2./maxnf2;
maxsf1=max(SFeature1(:));
SFeature1=SFeature1./maxsf1;
maxsf2=max(SFeature2(:));
SFeature2=SFeature2./maxsf2;
% create feature dataset here, we have taken only 1st two
features
% data11 = [NFeature1', NFeature2']; % Ham Points
% data22 = [SFeature1', SFeature2']; % Spam Points
%plot dataset
figure;
plot(data11(:,1),data11(:,2),'r.','MarkerSize',15)
hold on
plot(data22(:,1),data22(:,2),'b.','MarkerSize',15)
ezpolar(@(x)1);ezpolar(@(x)2);
axis equal
hold off

% prepare combined dataset
data33 = [data11;data22];

%label the dataset
 theclass = ones(600,1);
 theclass(1:300) = -1;


% Cross-validation data partition
 p = 0.25;
 CVP = cvpartition(theclass,'Holdout',p);
% Training sample indices
 isIdx = training(CVP);
% Test sample indices

 oosIdx = test(CVP);
% % Create an SVM template that specifies storing the support
vectors of the binary learners.
% % Pass it and the training data to fitcecoc to train the
model. Determine the training sample classification error.
% %Determine the amount of disk space that the ECOC-error
correcting output codes model consumes.
t = templateSVM('SaveSupportVectors',true);
MdlSV = fitcecoc(data33(isIdx,:),theclass(isIdx),'Learners',t);
isLoss = resubLoss(MdlSV)
predictedLabels = predict(MdlSV,data33(oosIdx,:));
predictedLabels = predict(classifier, testFeatures');
```

```
confMat = confusionmat(theclass(oosIdx), predictedLabels);
% % Convert confusion matrix into percentage form
confMat = bsxfun(@rdivide,confMat,sum(confMat,2))
% Display the mean accuracy
 mean(diag(confMat))
```

A.4. Function to Calculate Perimetric Complexity

```
function [ PerimetricComplexity] = GetPerimetricComplexity(img)
bw=im2bw(img);
bwp=bwperim(bw,8);
s1=sum(bw(:));
s2=sum(bwp(:));
PerimetricComplexity=(s2.*s2)./s1;
end
```

A.5. Function to Calculate Gabor Features

```
function featureVector = getgaborFeatures(img)
% GABORFEATURES extracts the Gabor features of an input image.
% It creates a column vector, consisting of the Gabor features
of the input
% image. The feature vectors are normalized to zero mean and
unit variance.
%
%
% Inputs:
%       img      :       Matrix of the input image
%       gaborArray   :        Gabor filters bank created
by the function gaborFilterBank
%       d1     :       The factor of downsampling along
rows.
%       d2     :       The factor of downsampling along
columns.
%
% Output:
%       featureVector       :    A column vector with length
(m*n*u*v)/(d1*d2).
%                      This vector is the Gabor feature
vector of an
%                      m by n image. u is the number of
scales and
```

```
%                          v is the number of orientations in
'gaborArray'.
%
%
% gaborArray = gaborFilterBank(5,8,39,39);   % Generates the
Gabor filter bank
u = 2; %5;
v = 4; %8;
gaborArray = gaborFilterBank(u,v,39,39);
d1=4;
d2=4;
% if size(img,3) == 3      % Check if the input image is
grayscale
%      warning('The input RGB image is converted to grayscale!')
%      img = rgb2gray(img);
%      img1 = img;
% end
img = double(img);
%% Filter the image using the Gabor filter bank
% Filter input image by each Gabor filter
[u,v] = size(gaborArray);
gaborResult = cell(u,v);
for i = 1:u
    for j = 1:v
        gaborResult{i,j} = imfilter(img, gaborArray{i,j});
    end
end
% % -------------------------------------------------
% subplot(2,2,1);
% imshow(img1);
% subplot(2,2,2);
% imshow(gaborResult{1,1});
% % -------------------------------------------------
% LPQhist = lpq(img1,3);
% subplot(2,2,3);
% bar(LPQhist);
% LPQhist = lpq(gaborResult{1,1},3);
% subplot(2,2,4);
% bar(LPQhist);
% %-------------------------------------------------
%% Create feature vector
% Extract feature vector from input image
featureVector = cell(u,v);
for i = 1:u
    for j = 1:v

        gaborResult1 = lpq(gaborResult{i,j},3);
        gaborAbs = abs(gaborResult1);
        gaborAbs = downsample(gaborAbs,d1);
```

```
        gaborAbs = downsample(gaborAbs.',d2);
        % Normalized to zero mean and unit variance. (if not
applicable, please comment this line)
%         gaborAbs = (gaborAbs-mean(gaborAbs))/std(gaborAbs,1);
        featureVector{i,j} =  gaborAbs;
    end
end
% % %% Show filtered images (Please comment this section if not
needed!)
% %
% % % % Show real parts of Gabor-filtered images
% % figure('NumberTitle','Off','Name','Real parts of Gabor
filters');
% % for i = 1:u
% %     for j = 1:v
% %         subplot(u,v,(i-1)*v+j)
% %         imshow(real(gaborResult{i,j}),[]);
% %     end
% % end
% %
% % % Show magnitudes of Gabor-filtered images
% % figure('NumberTitle','Off','Name','Magnitudes of Gabor
filters');
% % for i = 1:u
% %     for j = 1:v
% %         subplot(u,v,(i-1)*v+j)
% %         imshow(abs(gaborResult{i,j}),[]);
% %     end
% % end
```

A.6. Function to Calculate Gabor Filter Bank

```
function gaborArray = gaborFilterBank(u,v,m,n)
% GABORFILTERBANK generates a custum Gabor filter bank.
% It creates a u by v cell array, whose elements are m by n
matrices;
% each matrix being a 2-D Gabor filter.
%
%
% Inputs:
%     u       :        No. of scales (usually set to 5)
%     v       :        No. of orientations (usually set to
8)
%     m       :        No. of rows in a 2-D Gabor filter
(an odd integer number, usually set to 39)
```

```
%       n        :           No. of columns in a 2-D Gabor filter
(an odd integer number, usually set to 39)
%
% Output:
%       gaborArray: A u by v array, element of which are m by n
%                   matries; each matrix being a 2-D Gabor
filter
%
if (nargin ~= 4)     % Check correct number of arguments
    error('There must be four input arguments (Number of scales
and orientations and the 2-D size of the filter)!')
end
%% Create Gabor filters
% Create u*v gabor filters each being an m by n matrix
gaborArray = cell(u,v);
fmax = 0.25;
gama = sqrt(2);
eta = sqrt(2);
for i = 1:u

    fu = fmax/((sqrt(2))^(i-1));
    alpha = fu/gama;
    beta = fu/eta;

    for j = 1:v
        tetav = ((j-1)/v)*pi;
        gFilter = zeros(m,n);

        for x = 1:m
            for y = 1:n
                xprime = (x-((m+1)/2))*cos(tetav)+(y-
((n+1)/2))*sin(tetav);
                yprime = -(x-((m+1)/2))*sin(tetav)+(y-
((n+1)/2))*cos(tetav);
                gFilter(x,y) = (fu^2/(pi*gama*eta))*exp(-((alph
a^2)*(xprime^2)+(beta^2)*(yprime^2)))*exp(1i*2*pi*fu*xprime);
            end
        end
        gaborArray{i,j} = gFilter;

    end
end
% %% Show Gabor filters (Please comment this section if not
needed!)
%
% % Show magnitudes of Gabor filters:
% figure('NumberTitle','Off','Name','Magnitudes of Gabor
filters');
% for i = 1:u
```

```
%      for j = 1:v
%          subplot(u,v,(i-1)*v+j);
%          imshow(abs(gaborArray{i,j}),[]);
%      end
% end
%
% % Show real parts of Gabor filters:
% figure('NumberTitle','Off','Name','Real parts of Gabor
filters');
% for i = 1:u
%      for j = 1:v
%          subplot(u,v,(i-1)*v+j);
%          imshow(real(gaborArray{i,j}),[]);
%      end
% end
```

A.7. Function to Calculate Local Phase Quantization

```
function LPQdesc = lpq(img,winSize,decorr,freqestim,mode)
% Funtion LPQdesc=lpq(img,winSize,decorr,freqestim,mode)
computes the Local Phase Quantization (LPQ) descriptor
% for the input image img. Descriptors are calculated using
only valid pixels i.e. size(img)-(winSize-1).
%
% Inputs: (All empty or undefined inputs will be set to default
values)
% img = N*N uint8 or double, format gray scale image to be
analyzed.
% winSize = 1*1 double, size of the local window. winSize must
be odd number and greater or equal to 3 (default winSize=3).
% decorr = 1*1 double, indicates whether decorrelation is used
or not. Possible values are:
%                  0 -> no decorrelation,
%          (default) 1 -> decorrelation
% freqestim = 1*1 double, indicates which method is used for
local frequency estimation. Possible values are:
%          (default) 1 -> STFT with uniform window
(corresponds to basic version of LPQ)
%                    2 -> STFT with Gaussian window
(equals also to Gaussian quadrature filter pair)
%                    3 -> Gaussian derivative quadrature
filter pair.
% mode = 1*n char, defines the desired output type. Possible
choices are:
%          (default) 'nh' -> normalized histogram of LPQ
```

```
codewords (1*256 double vector, for which sum(result)==1)
%                  'h'  -> un-normalized histogram of LPQ
codewords (1*256 double vector)
%                  'im' -> LPQ codeword image ([size(img,1)-
r,size(img,2)-r] double matrix)
%
% Output:
% LPQdesc = 1*256 double or size(img)-(winSize-1) uint8, LPQ
descriptors histogram or LPQ code image (see "mode" above)
%% Default parameters
% Local window size
if nargin<2 || isempty(winSize)
    winSize=3; % default window size 3
end
% Decorrelation
if nargin<3 || isempty(decorr)
    decorr=1; % use decorrelation by default
end
rho=0.90; % Use correlation coefficient rho=0.9 as default
% Local frequency estimation (Frequency points used [alpha,0],
[0,alpha], [alpha,alpha], and [alpha,-alpha])
if nargin<4 || isempty(freqestim)
    freqestim=1; %use Short-Term Fourier Transform (STFT) with
uniform window by default
end
STFTalpha=1/winSize;  % alpha in STFT approaches (for Gaussian
derivative alpha=1)
sigmaS=(winSize-1)/4; % Sigma for STFT Gaussian window (applied
if freqestim==2)
sigmaA=8/(winSize-1); % Sigma for Gaussian derivative
quadrature filters (applied if freqestim==3)
% Output mode
if nargin<5 || isempty(mode)
    mode='nh'; % return normalized histogram as default
end
% Other
convmode='valid'; % Compute descriptor responses only on part
that have full neigborhood. Use 'same' if all pixels are
included (extrapolates image with zeros).
%% Check inputs
if size(img,3)~=1
%     error('Only gray scale image can be used as input');
    img = rgb2gray(img);
end
if winSize<3 || rem(winSize,2)~=1
   error('Window size winSize must be odd number and greater
than equal to 3');
end
if sum(decorr==[0 1])==0
```

```
    error('decorr parameter must be set to 0->no decorrelation
or 1->decorrelation. See help for details.');
end
if sum(freqestim==[1 2 3])==0
    error('freqestim parameter must be 1, 2, or 3. See help for
details.');
end
if sum(strcmp(mode,{'nh','h','im'}))==0
    error('mode must be nh, h, or im. See help for details.');
end
%% Initialize
img=double(img); % Convert image to double
r=(winSize-1)/2; % Get radius from window size
x=-r:r; % Form spatial coordinates in window
u=1:r; % Form coordinates of positive half of the Frequency
domain (Needed for Gaussian derivative)
%% Form 1-D filters
if freqestim==1% STFT uniform window
    % Basic STFT filters
    w0=(x*0+1);
    w1=exp(complex(0,-2*pi*x*STFTalpha));
    w2=conj(w1);

elseif freqestim==2% STFT Gaussian window (equals to Gaussian
quadrature filter pair)
    % Basic STFT filters
    w0=(x*0+1);
    w1=exp(complex(0,-2*pi*x*STFTalpha));
    w2=conj(w1);
    % Gaussian window
    gs=exp(-0.5*(x./sigmaS).^2)./(sqrt(2*pi).*sigmaS);

    % Windowed filters
    w0=gs.*w0;
    w1=gs.*w1;
    w2=gs.*w2;

    % Normalize to zero mean
    w1=w1-mean(w1);
    w2=w2-mean(w2);

elseif freqestim==3% Gaussian derivative quadrature filter pair
    % Frequency domain definition of filters
    G0=exp(-x.^2*(sqrt(2)*sigmaA)^2);
    G1=[zeros(1,length(u)),0,u.*exp(-u.^2*sigmaA^2)];

    % Normalize to avoid small numerical values (do not change
the phase response we use)
    G0=G0/max(abs(G0));
```

```
    G1=G1/max(abs(G1));

    % Compute spatial domain correspondences of the filters
    w0=real(fftshift(ifft(ifftshift(G0))));
    w1=fftshift(ifft(ifftshift(G1)));
    w2=conj(w1);

    % Normalize to avoid small numerical values (do not change
the phase response we use)
    w0=w0/max(abs([real(max(w0)),imag(max(w0))]));
    w1=w1/max(abs([real(max(w1)),imag(max(w1))]));
    w2=w2/max(abs([real(max(w2)),imag(max(w2))]));
end
%% Run filters to compute the frequency response in the four
points. Store real and imaginary parts separately
% Run first filter
filterResp=conv2(conv2(img,w0.',convmode),w1,convmode);
% Initilize frequency domain matrix for four frequency
coordinates (real and imaginary parts for each frequency).
freqResp=zeros(size(filterResp,1),size(filterResp,2),8);
% Store filter outputs
freqResp(:,:,1)=real(filterResp);
freqResp(:,:,2)=imag(filterResp);
% Repeat the procedure for other frequencies
filterResp=conv2(conv2(img,w1.',convmode),w0,convmode);
freqResp(:,:,3)=real(filterResp);
freqResp(:,:,4)=imag(filterResp);
filterResp=conv2(conv2(img,w1.',convmode),w1,convmode);
freqResp(:,:,5)=real(filterResp);
freqResp(:,:,6)=imag(filterResp);
filterResp=conv2(conv2(img,w1.',convmode),w2,convmode);
freqResp(:,:,7)=real(filterResp);
freqResp(:,:,8)=imag(filterResp);
% Read the size of frequency matrix
[freqRow,freqCol,freqNum]=size(freqResp);
%% If decorrelation is used, compute covariance matrix and
corresponding whitening transform
if decorr == 1
    % Compute covariance matrix (covariance between pixel
positions x_i and x_j is rho^||x_i-x_j||)
    [xp,yp]=meshgrid(1:winSize,1:winSize);
    pp=[xp(:) yp(:)];
    dd=dist(pp,pp');
    C=rho.^dd;

    % Form 2-D filters q1, q2, q3, q4 and corresponding 2-D
matrix operator M (separating real and imaginary parts)
    q1=w0.'*w1;
    q2=w1.'*w0;
```

```
    q3=w1.'*w1;
    q4=w1.'*w2;
    u1=real(q1); u2=imag(q1);
    u3=real(q2); u4=imag(q2);
    u5=real(q3); u6=imag(q3);
    u7=real(q4); u8=imag(q4);
    M=[u1(:)';u2(:)';u3(:)';u4(:)';u5(:)';u6(:)';u7(:)'
;u8(:)'];

    % Compute whitening transformation matrix V
    D=M*C*M';
    A=diag([1.000007 1.000006 1.000005 1.000004 1.000003
1.000002 1.000001 1]); % Use "random" (almost unit) diagonal
matrix to avoid multiple eigenvalues.
    [U,S,V]=svd(A*D*A);

    % In order to avoid any sign problems in SVM, force the
sign of the largest magnitude element in each singular vector
to be positive
    [~,ii]=max(abs(V),[],1);
    V=V*diag(ones(1,size(V,2))-2*double(V((ii+(0:(length(ii)-
1))*size(V,1)))<(-eps)));
    % Reshape frequency response
    freqResp=reshape(freqResp,[freqRow*freqCol,freqNum]);
    % Perform whitening transform
    freqResp=(V.'*freqResp.').';

    % Undo reshape
    freqResp=reshape(freqResp,[freqRow,freqCol,freqNum]);
end
%% Perform quantization and compute LPQ codewords
LPQdesc=zeros(freqRow,freqCol); % Initialize LPQ code word
image (size depends whether valid or same area is used)
for i=1:freqNum
    LPQdesc=LPQdesc+(double(freqResp(:,:,i))>0)*(2^(i-1));
end
%% Switch format to uint8 if LPQ code image is required as
output
if strcmp(mode,'im')
    LPQdesc=uint8(LPQdesc);
end
%% Histogram if needed
if strcmp(mode,'nh') || strcmp(mode,'h')
    LPQdesc=hist(LPQdesc(:),0:255);
end
%% Normalize histogram if needed
if strcmp(mode,'nh')
    LPQdesc=LPQdesc/sum(LPQdesc);
end
```

A.8. Function to Calculate Central Moments

```
function  [ M11,M02, M20,ecc ] = getcentralmoments(img)
%central moments
sz = size(img); %// assuming image is gray scale - 2D array
x = (1:sz(2));
y = (1:sz(1)).'; %'
x = x - mean(x);
y = y - mean(y);
M11 = sum(reshape(bsxfun(@times, bsxfun(@times, double(img),
x.^1), y.^1), [], 1));
M02 = sum(reshape(bsxfun(@times, bsxfun(@times, double(img),
x.^0), y.^2), [], 1));
M20 = sum(reshape(bsxfun(@times, bsxfun(@times, double(img),
x.^2), y.^0), [], 1));
ecc=((M20-M02)^2+4*M11.*M11)./(M20+M02)^2;
end
```

A.9. Function to Calculate Zernike Moments

```
function  [Z, AOH, PhiOH] = getzernikemoments(img)
% n=4;
% m=2;
% p = logical(not(img));
% [Z, AOH, PhiOH] = Zernikmoment(p,n,m);
end
```

A.10. Function to Calculate Zernike Moments

```
function [Z, A, Phi] = Zernikmoment(p,n,m)
% [Z, A, Phi] = Zernikmoment(p,n,m)
% where
%   p = input image N x N matrix (N should be an even number)
%   n = The order of Zernike moment (scalar)
%   m = The repetition number of Zernike moment (scalar)
% and
%   Z = Complex Zernike moment
%   A = Amplitude of the moment
%   Phi = phase (angle) of the moment (in degrees)
```

```
N = size(p,1);
x = 1:N; y = x;
[X,Y] = meshgrid(x,y);
R = sqrt((2.*X-N-1).^2+(2.*Y-N-1).^2)/N;
Theta = atan2((N-1-2.*Y+2),(2.*X-N+1-2));
R = (R<=1).*R;
Rad = radialpoly(R,n,m);      % get the radial polynomial

Product = p(x,y).*Rad.*exp(-1i*m*Theta);
Z = sum(Product(:));          % calculate the moments

cnt = nnz(R)+1;               % count the number of pixels inside
the unit circle
Z = (n+1)*Z/cnt;              % normalize the amplitude of
moments
A = abs(Z);                   % calculate the amplitude of the
moment
Phi = angle(Z)*180/pi;        % calculate the phase of the moment
(in degrees)
```

A.11. Function to Calculate Zernike Polynomials

```
function rad = radialpoly(r,n,m)
%    r = radius
%    n = the order of Zernike polynomial
%    m = the repetition of Zernike moment

rad = zeros(size(r));                        % Initialization
for s = 0:(n-abs(m))/2
  c = (-1)^s*factorial(n-s)/
(factorial(s)*factorial((n+abs(m))/2-s)*...
      factorial((n-abs(m))/2-s));
  rad = rad + c*r.^(n-2*s);
end
```

A.12. Function to Calculate 2d Autocorrelation

```
function B=autocorr2d(img)

[n m]=size(img);
% Divide by the size for normalization
```

```
Img1=abs(fftshift(ifft2(fft2(img).*conj(fft2(img))))./(n*m);
figure, surf(Img1);
shading interp;
```

A.13. Function to Calculate Color Coherence Vector

```
function CCV1 = getCCV(img,coherentPrec, numberOfColors)
%Input:
%img: RGB Image
%Optional Input:
%coherentPrec: The percentage of the image size to consider a
component's pixels are coherent (default = 1%)
 %numberOfColors: The number of different colors in the Color
Coherence Vector (default = 27 colors).
 %                            Note it'll be changed a
little bit to ensure the same different values for RGB channel
 %
%Output:
%CCV: a (2*numberOfColors) matrix represents your image. This
can be used for matching.
    if ~exist('coherentPrec','var')
        coherentPrec = 1;
    end
    if ~exist('numberOfColors','var')
        numberOfColors = 128; %27
    end
    CCV = zeros(2,numberOfColors);
    CCV1 = zeros(1,numberOfColors);

    Gaus = fspecial('gaussian',[5 5],2);
    img = imfilter(img,Gaus,'same');

    [img, updNumOfPix]= discretizeColors(img,numberOfColors);

    imgSize = (size(img,1)*size(img,2));
    thresh = int32((coherentPrec/100) *imgSize);

    for i=0:updNumOfPix-1
        BW = img==i;
        CC = bwconncomp(BW);
        compsSize = cellfun(@numel,CC.PixelIdxList);
        incoherent = sum(compsSize(compsSize>=thresh));
        CCV(:,i+1) = [incoherent; ...
            sum(compsSize) - incoherent];
        CCV1(:,i+1)=[sum(compsSize) - incoherent];
```

```
        end
end
```

A.14. Function to Calculate Color Saturation

```
function [ colsat ] = colorSaturation(img)

ss=size(img);
tpixels=ss(1)*ss(2);
count=0;
for i=1:ss(1)
    for j=1:ss(2)
        tmp=max(img(i,j,:))-min(img(i,j,:));
        if tmp>=50
            count=count+1;
        end
    end
end
colsat=count./tpixels;

end
```

A.15. Function to Calculate Fourier Mellin Coefficient

```
function [ wcoeff ] = fouriermellin(gx2)

SizeX = size(gx2, 1);
SizeY = size(gx2, 2);
FA = fftshift(fft2(gx2));
IA = hipass_filter(size(gx2, 1),size(gx2,2)).*abs(FA);
L1 = transformImage(IA, SizeX, SizeY, SizeX, SizeY, 'nearest',
size(IA) / 2, 'valid');
THETA_F1 = fft2(L1);
a1 = angle(THETA_F1);
a2 = abs(THETA_F1);
w = 1./var(a2);
[wcoeff,score,latent,tsquared,explained] = pca(a1,...
'VariableWeights',w);
coefforth = diag(sqrt(w))*wcoeff;

end
```

A.16. Function to Calculate Log Polar Transform

```
function [r,g,b] = transformImage(A, Ar, Ac, Nrho, Ntheta,
Method, Center, Shape)
% Performs Log Polar Transform
% Inputs:   A       the input image
%           Nrho    the desired number of rows of transformed
image
%           Ntheta  the desired number of columns of
transformed image
%           Method  interpolation method
(nearest,bilinear,bicubic)
%           Center  origin of input image
%           Shape   output size (full,valid)
%           Class   storage class of A

global rho;

theta = linspace(0,2*pi,Ntheta+1); theta(end) = [];

switch Shape
case 'full'
    corners = [1 1;Ar 1;Ar Ac;1 Ac];
    d = max(sqrt(sum((repmat(Center(:)',4,1)-corners).^2,2)));
case 'valid'
    d = min([Ac-Center(1) Center(1)-1 Ar-Center(2)
Center(2)-1]);
end
minScale = 1;
rho = logspace(log10(minScale),log10(d),Nrho)';  % default
'base 10' logspace - play with d to change the scale of the log
axis

% convert polar coordinates to cartesian coordinates and center
xx = rho*cos(theta) + Center(1);
yy = rho*sin(theta) + Center(2);

if nargout==3
  if strcmp(Method,'nearest'), % Nearest neighbor interpolation
    r=interp2(A(:,:,1),xx,yy,'nearest');
    g=interp2(A(:,:,2),xx,yy,'nearest');
    b=interp2(A(:,:,3),xx,yy,'nearest');
  elseif strcmp(Method,'bilinear'), % Linear interpolation
    r=interp2(A(:,:,1),xx,yy,'linear');
    g=interp2(A(:,:,2),xx,yy,'linear');
    b=interp2(A(:,:,3),xx,yy,'linear');
  elseif strcmp(Method,'bicubic'), % Cubic interpolation
```

```
     r=interp2(A(:,:,1),xx,yy,'cubic');
     g=interp2(A(:,:,2),xx,yy,'cubic');
     b=interp2(A(:,:,3),xx,yy,'cubic');
   else
     error(['Unknown interpolation method: ',method]);
   end
   % any pixels outside, pad with black
   mask= (xx>Ac) | (xx<1) | (yy>Ar) | (yy<1);
   r(mask)=0;
   g(mask)=0;
   b(mask)=0;
else
  if strcmp(Method,'nearest'), % Nearest neighbor interpolation
    r=interp2(A,xx,yy,'nearest');
  elseif strcmp(Method,'bilinear'), % Linear interpolation
    r=interp2(A,xx,yy,'linear');
  elseif strcmp(Method,'bicubic'), % Cubic interpolation
    r=interp2(A,xx,yy,'cubic');
  else
    error(['Unknown interpolation method: ',method]);
  end
  % any pixels outside warp, pad with black
  mask= (xx>Ac) | (xx<1) | (yy>Ar) | (yy<1);
  r(mask)=0;
end
```

A.17. Function to Calculate Dualtree Complex Discrete Wavelet Transform

```
function w = cplxdual2D(x)

% Dual-Tree Complex 2D Discrete Wavelet Transform
%
% USAGE:
%   w = cplxdual2D(x, J, Faf, af)
% INPUT:
%   x - 2-D array
%   J - number of stages
%   Faf{i}: first stage filters for tree i
%   af{i}:  filters for remaining stages on tree i
% OUTPUT:
%   w{j}{i}{d1}{d2} - wavelet coefficients
%       j = 1..J (scale)
%       i = 1 (real part); i = 2 (imag part)
%       d1 = 1,2; d2 = 1,2,3 (orientations)
```

```
%    w{J+1}{m}{n} - lowpass coefficients
%        d1 = 1,2; d2 = 1,2

Faf{1} = [
                        0                        0
  -0.08838834764832    -0.01122679215254
   0.08838834764832     0.01122679215254
   0.69587998903400     0.08838834764832
   0.69587998903400     0.08838834764832
   0.08838834764832    -0.69587998903400
  -0.08838834764832     0.69587998903400
   0.01122679215254    -0.08838834764832
   0.01122679215254    -0.08838834764832
                        0                        0
 ];

Fsf{1} = af{1}(end:-1:1,:);

Faf{2} = [
   0.01122679215254                        0
   0.01122679215254                        0
  -0.08838834764832    -0.08838834764832
   0.08838834764832    -0.08838834764832
   0.69587998903400     0.69587998903400
   0.69587998903400    -0.69587998903400
   0.08838834764832     0.08838834764832
  -0.08838834764832     0.08838834764832
                   0     0.01122679215254
                   0    -0.01122679215254
];

Fsf{2} = af{2}(end:-1:1,:);


af{1} = [
   0.03516384000000                        0
                   0                        0
  -0.08832942000000    -0.11430184000000
   0.23389032000000                        0
   0.76027237000000     0.58751830000000
   0.58751830000000    -0.76027237000000
                   0     0.23389032000000
  -0.11430184000000     0.08832942000000
                   0                        0
                   0    -0.03516384000000
 ];

af{2} = [
                   0    -0.03516384000000
```

```
                        0                         0
     -0.11430184000000       0.08832942000000
                        0       0.23389032000000
      0.58751830000000      -0.76027237000000
      0.76027237000000       0.58751830000000
      0.23389032000000                         0
     -0.08832942000000      -0.11430184000000
                        0                         0
      0.03516384000000                         0
];

sf{1} = af{1}(end:-1:1,:);

sf{2} = af{2}(end:-1:1,:);

% normalization
[x1 w{1}{1}] = afb2D(x, Faf{1});
for k = 2:J
    [x1 w{k}{1}] = afb2D(x1, af{1});
end
w{J+1}{1} = x1;

[x2 w{1}{2}] = afb2D(x, Faf{2});
for k = 2:J
    [x2 w{k}{2}] = afb2D(x2, af{2});
end
w{J+1}{2} = x2;

for k = 1:J
    for m = 1:3
        [w{k}{1}{m} w{k}{2}{m}] = pm(w{k}{1}{m},w{k}{2}{m});
    end
end
```

A.18. Function to Calculate 2D Analysis Filter Bank

```
function [lo, hi] = afb2D(x, af1, af2)

% 2D Analysis Filter Bank
%
% USAGE:
%    [lo, hi] = afb2D(x, af1, af2);
% INPUT:
%    x - N by M matrix
%        1) M, N are both even
```

```
%         2) M >= 2*length(af1)
%         3) N >= 2*length(af2)
%   af1 - analysis filters for columns
%   af2 - analysis filters for rows
% OUTPUT:
%    lo - lowpass subband
%    hi{1} - 'lohi' subband
%    hi{2} - 'hilo' subband
%    hi{3} - 'hihi' subband
if nargin < 3
   af2 = af1;
end

% filter along columns
[L, H] = afb2D_A(x, af1, 1);

% filter along rows
[lo,   hi{1}] = afb2D_A(L, af2, 2);
[hi{2}, hi{3}] = afb2D_A(H, af2, 2);
```

A.19. Function to Calculate Color Histogram Distance

```
function [colorHistogramDist1] = getcolorHistogramDist(Template
SpamImg,x1)

s1=size(TemplateSpamImg);
x2 = imresize(x1, [s1(1) s1(2)]);

[Rcounts1,R_vector1] = imhist(TemplateSpamImg(:,:,1),4);
Rcounts1=Rcounts1./(s1(1)*s1(2));
[Gcounts1,G_vector1] = imhist(TemplateSpamImg(:,:,2),4);
Gcounts1=Gcounts1./(s1(1)*s1(2));
[Bcounts1,B_vector1] = imhist(TemplateSpamImg(:,:,3),4);
Bcounts1=Bcounts1./(s1(1)*s1(2));

[Rcounts,R_vector] = imhist(x2(:,:,1),4);
Rcounts=Rcounts./(s1(1)*s1(2));
[Gcounts,G_vector] = imhist(x2(:,:,2),4);
Gcounts=Gcounts./(s1(1)*s1(2));
[Bcounts,B_vector] = imhist(x2(:,:,3),4);
Bcounts=Bcounts./(s1(1)*s1(2));

temp=sum([[(abs(Rcounts1-Rcounts)) (abs(Gcounts1-Gcounts))
(abs(Bcounts1-Bcounts))]]);
colorHistogramDist1=sum(temp)./3;
```

```
end
```

A.20. Function to Calculate Energy Difference Between Low Frequency and High Frequency Subband

```
function [energydiff] = getenergydiffLFandHF(x)

s1=size(x);
H = lpfilter('gaussian', s1(1), s1(2), 0.05*s1(1));
F=fft2(double(x),size(H,1),size(H,2));
LPF_x=real(ifft2(H.*F));

H1 = hpfilter('gaussian', s1(1), s1(2), 0.05*s1(1));
F1=fft2(double(x),size(H1,1),size(H1,2));
HPF_x=real(ifft2(H1.*F1));

e1=(LPF_x.*LPF_x);
e2=(HPF_x.*HPF_x);
e3=e1-e2;
energydiff=sum(e3(:));

end
```

A.21. Function to Calculate High Frequency Subband

```
function H = hpfilter(type, M, N, D0, n)
%HPFILTER Computes frequency domain highpass filters
%   H = HPFILTER(TYPE, M, N, D0, n) creates the transfer
function of
%   a highpass filter, H, of the specified TYPE and size
(M-by-N).
%   Valid values for TYPE, D0, and n are:
%
%   'ideal'     Ideal highpass filter with cutoff frequency D0.
n
%               need not be supplied.  D0 must be positive
%
%   'btw'       Butterworth highpass filter of order n, and
cutoff D0.
%               The default value for n is 1.0.  D0 must be
positive.
```

```
%
%    'gaussian'  Gaussian highpass filter with cutoff (standard
deviation)
% D0.  n need not be supplied.  D0 must be positive.
%

% The transfer function Hhp of a highpass filter is 1 - Hlp,
% where Hlp is the transfer function of the corresponding
lowpass
% filter.  Thus, we can use function lpfilter to generate
highpass
% filters.

if nargin == 4
   n = 1; % Default value of n.
end

% Generate highpass filter.
Hlp = lpfilter(type, M, N, D0, n);
H = 1 - Hlp;
```

A.22. Function to Calculate Low Frequency Subband

```
function H = lpfilter(type, M, N, D0, n)
%LPFILTER Computes frequency domain lowpass filters
%   H = LPFILTER(TYPE, M, N, D0, n) creates the transfer
function of
%   a lowpass filter, H, of the specified TYPE and size
(M-by-N).  To
%   view the filter as an image or mesh plot, it should be
centered
%   using H = fftshift(H).
%
%   Valid values for TYPE, D0, and n are:
%
%   'ideal'    Ideal lowpass filter with cutoff frequency D0.
n need
%              not be supplied.  D0 must be positive
%
%   'btw'      Butterworth lowpass filter of order n, and
cutoff D0.
%              The default value for n is 1.0.  D0 must be
positive.
%
%   'gaussian' Gaussian lowpass filter with cutoff (standard
```

```
deviation)
%              D0.  n need not be supplied.  D0 must be
positive.

% Use function dftuv to set up the meshgrid arrays needed for
% computing the required distances.
[U, V] = dftuv(M, N);

% Compute the distances D(U, V).
D = sqrt(U.^2 + V.^2);

% Begin fiter computations.
switch type
case 'ideal'
   H = double(D <=D0);
case 'btw'
   if nargin == 4
      n = 1;
   end
   H = 1./(1 + (D./D0).^(2*n));
case 'gaussian'
   H = exp(-(D.^2)./(2*(D0^2)));
otherwise
   error('Unknown filter type.')
end
```

A.23. Function to Plot Distribution

```
figure,
hist(NFeature1,100,'-r')
hold on
h = findobj(gca,'Type','patch');
h.FaceColor = [0.8 0.8 0.1];
h.EdgeColor = 'r';
hist(SFeature1,100)
xlabel('Distribution of Grayscale-mean in Spam and Ham')
```

A.24. Function to Plot Color Histogram

```
%color histogram
image1=x1;
```

```
    Red = image1(:,:,1);
    Green = image1(:,:,2);
    Blue = image1(:,:,3);
    %Get histValues for each channel
    [yRed, x] = imhist(Red);
    [yGreen, x] = imhist(Green);
    [yBlue, x] = imhist(Blue);
    %Plot them together in one plot
    plot(x, yRed, 'Red', x, yGreen, 'Green', x, yBlue, 'Blue');
ylabel('Distribution of RGB Bands');
xlabel('Color Histogram: Sample Spam Image');
```

B. TOOLS AND TECHNIQUES

B.1. Points and Vectors

Point (P) is a position specified by coordinate values i.e. ordered pair (x,y); while a vector (V), is defined as the difference between two point positions (P_1) and (P_2) as in Equation (1).

$$V = P_2 - P_1 = (x_2 - x_1, y_2 - y_1) = (V_x, V_y) \tag{1}$$

where, the Cartesian elements V_x and V_y are the projections of V onto the x and y axes.

A vector can be expressed as a directed line segment with magnitude $|V| = \sqrt{V_x^2 + V_y^2}$ (Pythagoras theorem) and direction/angular displacement from x axis $\alpha = \tan^{-1}\left(\dfrac{V_y}{V_x}\right)$.

Sum of two vectors V_1 and V_2 is given as in Equation (2).

$$V_1 + V_2 = (V_{1x} + V_{2x}, V_{1y} + V_{2y}) \tag{2}$$

Scalar multiplication of 2D vector by scalar parameter α is given as in Equation (3).

$$\alpha V = (\alpha V_x, \alpha V_y) \tag{3}$$

Scalar/dot/inner product of two vectors V_1 and V_2 is given as in Equation (4).

$$V_1 \bullet V_2 = |V_1||V_2|\cos\theta = V_{1x}V_{2x} + V_{1y}V_{2y} \tag{4}$$

where, θ is the angle between the two vectors.

Dot products are commutative, means $V_1 \bullet V_2 = V_2 \bullet V_1$ and distributive with respect to vector addition, means $V_1 \bullet (V_2 + V_3) = V_1 \bullet V_2 + V_2 \bullet V_1$.

Vector Product or multiplication of two vectors V_1 and V_2 is given as in Equation (5).

$$V_1 \times V_2 = (V_{1y}V_{2x} - V_{1x}V_{2y}) \tag{5}$$

The cross product of a vector with itself is zero i.e. $V_1 \times V_1 = 0$ and also, the cross product is not commutative, i.e. $V_1 \times V_2 \neq V_2 \times V_1$ or $V_1 \times V_2 = -(V_2 \times V_1)$. However, cross product is distributive over vector addition i.e. $V_1 \times (V_2 + V_3) = V_1 \times V_2 + V_2 \times V_1$.

B.2. Matrices

A $m \times n$ matrix, A_{mn} is a rectangular array of elements given as in Equation (6), where a_{ij} represent the element at i^{th} row and j^{th} column.

$$A_{mn} = \begin{bmatrix} a_{11} & a_{12} & \cdots & a_{1n} \\ a_{21} & a_{22} & \cdots & a_{2n} \\ \cdot & & \vdots & \vdots \\ \cdot & \vdots & \vdots & \vdots \\ a_{m1} & a_{m2} & \cdots & a_{mn} \end{bmatrix} \tag{6}$$

A matrix with a single row is called as row vector and with a single column is called as column vector.

For scalar matrix multiplication, multiply each element a_{ij} by a scalar value. For matrix addition or subtraction, both matrices A_{mn} and B_{mn} should have the same number of rows and same number of columns. The sum is calculated by adding the corresponding elements of both matrices. To multiply matrix A_{mn} and B_{np}, the number of columns in A must be equal to the number of rows in B and the elements of product matrix $C = A \times B$ is given as in Equation (7).

$$c_{ij} = \sum_{k=1}^{n} a_{ik}.b_{kj} \tag{7}$$

Matrix multiplication is not commutative i.e. $A{\times}B{\neq}B{\times}A$ however, matrix multiplication is distributive with respect to matrix addition $A{\times}(B{+}C){=}A{\times}B{+}A{\times}C$.

The transpose of a matrix A^T is obtained by interchanging rows and columns of matrix A_{mn} and the transpose of matrix product is as given in Equation (8).

$$(AB)^T = B^T A^T \tag{8}$$

The determinant of 2×2 matrix is given as in Equation (9). Calculating determinants for large matrices can be done more efficiently using certain numerical methods.

$$\begin{vmatrix} a_{11} & a_{12} \\ a_{21} & a_{22} \end{vmatrix} = a_{11}a_{22} - a_{12}a_{21} \tag{9}$$

The inverse of an $n{\times}n$ square matrix A is denoted as A^{-1} and such that, $A^{-1}A = AA^{-1} = I$ where, I is identity matrix containing all diagonal elements of value=1 and all other elements=0.

Elements for the inverse matrix A^{-1} can be calculated from the elements of A as in Equation (10).

$$a_{jk}^{-1} = \frac{(-1)^{j+k} \det(A_{kj})}{\det(A)} \tag{10}$$

where a_{jk}^{-1} is the element in the jth row and k^{th} column of A^{-1}, and A_{kj} is the $(n{-}1)$ by $(n{-}1)$ sub matrix obtained by deleting the kth row and j^{th} column of matrix A.

B.3. Introduction to Images

B.3.1. What are Images?

An image is an artifact representing visual perception for e.g. a two-dimensional picture, which has a similar appearance to some physical object. Images may be two-dimensional, such as a photograph or three-dimensional, such as a statue. Natural objects such as human eye or optical devices such as cameras, can capture an image.

B.3.2. Types of Images

- **Binary Image:** Each pixel takes only two values - just black or white. We need only one bit per pixel hence binary images are efficient for storage. Figure 1 shows an example of 16x16 binary image containing total 16x16=256 pixels and each pixel is denoted by 1 bit only. Hence total number of bits required to store this image=256 bits only; which is 32bytes (Note that 1byte refers to 8bits).
- **Greyscale Image:** In these type of images, each pixel is a shade of grey, normally from black (denoted by value 0) to white (denoted by value 255). Each pixel is represented by eight bits i.e. exactly by one byte. Figure 2 shows an example of 32x32 greyscale image containing total 32x32=1024 pixels and each pixel is denoted by 8 bits. Hence total number of bits required to store this image=1024x8=8192 bits only; which is 1024bytes or 1KiloBytes.
- **Color Image:** In these types of images, each pixel is a represented by a color; which is described by the amount of Red, Green and Blue components in it. The value of each of these components range from 0-255, this gives a total of 256x256x256=16,777,216 different possible colors. Since the total number of bits required for each pixel is 24 bits. A color image hence consist of a stack of three matrices

Figure 1. A Binary Image

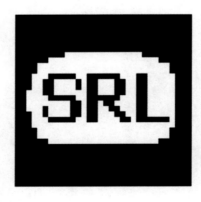

Figure 2. A Greyscale Image

depicting RGB planes; representing the red, green and blue values for each pixel. Figure 3 shows an example of color image, containing total 32x32=1024 pixels and each pixel is denoted by 24 bits. Hence total number of bits required to store this image=1024x24=24576 bits only; which is 3072bytes or 3KiloBytes approximately.

- **Indexed Image:** Most colour images only have a small subset of the more than sixteen million possible colours. For convenience of storage and file handling, the image has an associated colour map/palette,

Figure 3. A Color Image

containing a list of all the colors used in that image. Each pixel has a value which refers to an index to the colour in the map. If an image has 256 colours or less, for then the index values will only require one byte each to store. Compuserve GIF format, allow only 256 colours or fewer in each image.

B.3.3. What is Image Processing?

Image processing usually refers to digital image processing. It is processing of images using mathematical operations or standard signal-processing techniques. It is carried out on images to improve its pictorial information for human interpretation or to render it more suitable for autonomous machine perception. For e.g. enhancing the edges of an image to make it appear sharper, removing noise/blur from an image, obtaining edges/objects etc.

It generally includes acquiring an image using camera/scanner, preprocessing to enhance contrast/remove noise/blur, segmentation to identify region/object, extracting features/ assigning labels to the objects etc.

B.3.4. Applications of Image Processing

Image processing has a huge range of applications; in many areas like patient data analysis based on medical/ X-rays/MRI/CT scan images, study of satellite/ aerial views of land, automatic attendance system based on face recognition, security applications like biometric recognition system, law enforcement applications like Fingerprint analysis etc.

B.4. Color Models

B.4.1. RGB Color Model

RGB color model is most commonly used color model. It defines a color by giving the intensity level of red, green and blue light that mix together to create a pixel on the display. With most of today's displays, the intensity of each color can vary from 0 to 255, which gives 16,777,216 different colors. Table 1 shows some example colors based on their red, green and blue intensity values:

Table 1. Example colors created using RGB color model

Color	Red	Green	Blue
Red	255	0	0
Green	0	255	0
Blue	0	0	255
Yellow	255	255	0
Cyan	0	255	255
Magenta	255	0	255
White	255	255	255
Black	0	0	0

B.4.2. HSL (Hue, Saturation, and Lightness) Color Model

HSL color model is based on intuitive color parameters, being derived from the RGB color cube. It is represented by a double hexagonal pyramid as can be seeing in Figure 4.

Hue (H) specifies an angle about the vertical axis of the pyramid, varying from 0°, that corresponds to the red, to 360°. The parameter H possesses indefinite value for the gray scale which varies from black to white. Saturation (S) is measured along the horizontal radius of the pyramid and specifies the relative purity of the color. This parameter varies from 0 (gray scale) to 1 (pure colors). Lightness (L), measured along the vertical axis, possesses value 0 for black and 1 for white. It specifies the amount of light in the color.

B.4.3. HSV (Hue, Saturation, and Lightness) Color Model

HSL color model is as shown in Figure 5; where *hue* (H) of a color refers to which pure color it resembles. All tints, tones and shades of red have the same hue. Hues are described by a number that specifies the position of the corresponding pure color on the color wheel, as a fraction between 0 and 1. Value 0 refers to red; 1/6 is yellow; 1/3 is green; and so forth around the color wheel. The *saturation* (S) of a color describes how white the color is. A pure red is fully saturated, with a saturation of 1; tints of red have saturations less than 1; and white has a saturation of 0. The *value* (V) of a color, also called its *lightness*, describes how dark the color is. A value of 0 is black, with increasing lightness moving away from black. The outer edge of the top of the cone is the color wheel, with all the pure colors. The H parameter

Figure 4. HSL Color Model

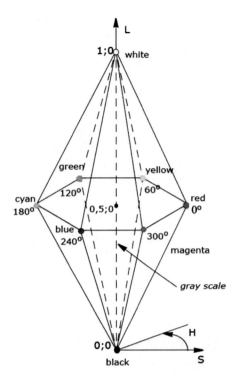

describes the angle around the wheel. The S (saturation) is zero for any color on the axis of the cone; the center of the top circle is white. An increase in the value of S corresponds to a movement away from the axis. The V (value or lightness) is zero for black. An increase in the value of V corresponds to a movement away from black and toward the top of the cone.

B.5. Transform Domain Techniques

This section introduces different transforms that are generally used in audio watermarking algorithms. The features of different transform domains which are exploited during watermarking process are also described.

Discrete Wavelet Transform (DWT)

The discrete wavelet transform (DWT) decompose hierarchically a given audio signal into a series of successively lower frequency approximation

Figure 5. HSV Color Model

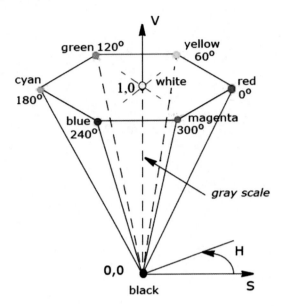

subbands and their associated detail subbands. The Lth level DWT decomposition of an audio signal $X(k)$ generates L^{th} level approximate part A_k^L along with detail parts $D_k^1, D_k^2, ..., D_k^L$ at level 1 to L.

Discrete Cosine Transform (DCT)

For a given signal sequence $x(0)$; $x(1)$; …; $x(N–1)$ containing N points, 1D discrete cosine transform (DCT) coefficients are given by Equation (11) and inverse DCT is given by Equation (12) respectively.

$$X(k) = \alpha_k \sum_{n=0}^{N-1} x(n) \cos\left(\frac{\pi(2n+1)k}{2N}\right), 0 \leq k \leq N-1 \tag{11}$$

$$x(n) = \sum_{n=0}^{N-1} \alpha_k X(k) \cos\left(\frac{\pi(2n+1)k}{2N}\right), 0 \leq n \leq N-1 \tag{12}$$

where,

$$\alpha_k = \begin{cases} \sqrt{\dfrac{1}{N}} \ for & k = 0 \\[3mm] \sqrt{\dfrac{2}{N}} \ for & k = 1, 2, ..., N-1 \end{cases}$$

The energy compaction property of DCT is useful for extraction of signal features. DCT concentrates energy in first few DCT coefficients. The first DCT coefficient is also known as DC coefficient.

Discrete Fourier Transform (DFT)

The N point discrete Fourier transform (DFT) of audio sequence $x(0)$; $x(1)$; ...; $x(N–1)$ containing N points, is given by Equation (13) and inverse DFT is given by Equation (14) respectively.

$$F_x(k) = \sum_{n=0}^{N-1} x(n) \exp\left(\frac{-j2\pi nk}{2N}\right), 0 \le k \le N-1 \tag{13}$$

$$x(n) = \frac{1}{N} \sum_{k=0}^{N-1} F_x(k) \exp\left(\frac{j2\pi nk}{2N}\right), 0 \le n \le N-1 \tag{14}$$

Singular Value Decomposition (SVD)

The singular value decomposition (SVD) is a factorization of a real or complex matrix. Generally, SVD is used along with any other transform domain techniques like DCT, DFT, DWT etc. to extract the robust image features. The singular value decomposition of an arbitrary matrix A_{mn} of rank r is given by Equation (15).

$A = USV^T$ (15) where, U and V are orthogonal $m \times m$ and $n \times n$ matrices, respectively; and $S = diag(A)$ is a diagonal matrix of singular values which are arranged in decreasing order. Singular values represent algebraic properties of the signal. The largest singular value is invariant to common signal processing operations. Adding a small perturbation to the matrix, do not cause large variance of its singular values. These properties make singular values useful for extracting robust features.

B.6. Machine Learning Techniques

Learning is used in the design of all classifiers that incorporates information from training samples. Learning process reduces the decision error on a set of training data. A range of *gradient descent* algorithms can alter a classifier's parameters in order to reduce an error measure. Learning can be supervised, unsupervised or rein enforced.

1. **Supervised Learning:** In supervised learning, a teacher provides a category label or cost for each pattern in a training set, and we seek to reduce the sum of the costs for these patterns.

2. **Unsupervised Learning:** In *unsupervised learning* or *clustering* there is no explicit teacher, and the system forms clusters of the input patterns which, is always defined explicitly or implicitly in the clustering system itself, and given a particular set of patterns or cost function, different clustering algorithms lead to different clusters.

3. **Reinforcement Learning:** The most typical way to train a classifier is to present an input, compute its tentative category label, and use the known target category label to improve the classifier. In *reinforcement learning* or *learning with a critic*, no desired category signal is given; critic instead, the only teaching feedback is that the tentative category is right or wrong. This is analogous to a critic who merely states that something is right or wrong, but does not say specifically *how* it is wrong. Thus only binary feedback is given to the classifier; reinforcement learning also describes the case where a single scalar signal, say some number between 0 and 1, is given by the teacher. It is most common that such reinforcement is binary — either the tentative decision is correct or it is not. If given problem involves just two categories and equal costs for errors, then learning with a critic is equivalent to standard supervised learning.

B.7. Bayesian Decision Theory

This fundamental statistical approach is based on quantifying the tradeoffs between various classification decisions using probability and the costs that accompany such decisions. It makes the assumption that the decision problem is posed in probabilistic terms, and that all of the relevant probability values are known. Let either the given image I is ham i.e. $I=w_1$ or spam $I=w_2$. Because the state of given image I is so unpredictable, we consider I to be a variable that must be described probabilistically. There is some *a priori probability* $P(wi_1)$ that the image is ham, and some prior probability $P(w_2)$ that the image is spam. If we assume there are no other types of image relevant here, then $P(w_1)+P(w_2)=1$. These prior probabilities reflect our prior knowledge of how likely we are to get a ham or spam before the image actually received in mail box. Then decision rule can be set such that, decide w_1 if $P(w_1)>P(w_2)$; otherwise decide w_2. This rule makes sense if we are to judge just one image, but if we are to judge many images then using this rule repeatedly may seem a bit strange.

Let I be a continuous random variable. Then $P(I|w_1)$ and $P(I|w_2)$ will be the class-conditional probability density function of I, given that it is spam or ham respectively. Then the joint probability density of finding a given image that is in category w_j *and* has feature value I can be written two ways: $P(I,w_1)= P(I|w_j)P(w_j)= P(w_j|I)P(I)$. Rearranging the terms gives, the Bayes Formula as in Equation (16).

$$P(w_j \mid I) = \frac{P(I \mid w_j)P(w_j)}{P(I)} \tag{16}$$

By observing the value of I, we can convert the prior probability $P(w_j)$ to the a posteriori probability $P(w_j|I)$ where, $P(I|w_j)$ is the likelihood of w_j with respect to I and $P(I)$ is the evidence factor. In short, we can say, as in Equation (B.17).

$$Posterior = \frac{likelihood \times prior}{evidence} \tag{17}$$

Decide w_1 if $P(w_1|I)>P(w_2|I)$; otherwise decide w_2.

B.8. Support Vector Machines (SVM)

Support vector machines (SVM) relies on preprocessing the data to represent feature set in a high dimension - typically much higher than the original feature space. With an appropriate nonlinear mapping to a sufficiently high dimension, data from two categories can always be separated by a hyper plane. For each of the n patterns, $k=1,2,\ldots,n$ we let $z_k=\pm1$, according to whether pattern k is in w_1 or w_2. A linear discriminant in an augmented y space is $g(y)=a^t y$. Where, both the weight vector and the transformed pattern vector are augmented (by $a_0 = w_0$ and $y_0 = 1$, respectively). Thus a separating hyperplane insures $z_k g(Y_k) \geq 1$, $k=1,2,\ldots,n$.

The goal in training a Support Vector Machine is to find the optimal separating hyper plane with the largest margin (b)- distance from the decision hyperplane. i.e. $\dfrac{z_k g(Y_k)}{\|a\|} \geq b, k = 1,2,\ldots,n$ Larger the margin, better will be the generalization of the classifier. The support vectors are transformed patterns that determine the margin; they are informally the hardest patterns to classify, and the most informative ones for designing the classifier. An upper bound on expected error rate of the classifier depends linearly up on the expected number of support vectors.

B.9. Decision Trees

A Decision Tree is a finite tree structure with branches representing the tests, and the leaves denoting the categories. The classification is done by expanding from root to leaf in the tree, and only selecting conditions in branches that are evaluated as true. Evaluations are repeated until a leaf is reached, assigning the document to the category that denotes the leaf reached. There are many algorithms used for computing the learning tree. The most popular ones are ID3, C4.5 and C5 (Meghali Das and Vijay Prasad, 2014).

B.10. K-Nearest Neighbors (kNN)

k-Nearest Neighbors algorithm (k-NN) is a non-parametric method used for classification and regression. The input consists of the k closest training examples in the feature space. In k-NN classification, the output is a class membership. An object is classified by a majority vote of its neighbors, with the object being assigned to the class most common among its k nearest neighbors (k is a positive integer, typically small). In k-NN regression, the output is the property value for the object. This value is the average of the values of its k nearest neighbors.

B.11. Feature Scoring

Before applying spam text classification, sample spam images need to be converted from text form to vector space representation in matrix form where each row represents a spam image sample and each column represents the features. The total number of columns is the total number of features extracted from the documents.

To enable the classifier to effectively differentiate between various classes, feature scoring is done to give a numerical value to each of these features. Various techniques are used for feature scoring. Some of the techniques used by us in the paper are defined as follows.

B.11.1. Document Frequency (DF)

Document frequency of a feature gives the number of documents the feature occurs in a class of documents, (Salton, Gerard, and Christopher Buckley, 1988) and is given by Equation (18).

$$DF\left(f_i, C_j\right) = \frac{\lg|C_p|}{\lg|C_j|} \tag{18}$$

where,

(fi): Document frequency of the ith feature in jth class of documents.
Cp: Number of documents of class j which contain the feature.
Cj: Number of documents of class j
i: Index of the feature extracted (i∈ N), N is the total number of features.
j: Number of classes ie. benign and different malware families.

B.11.2. Bi-Normal Separation (BNS)

BNS measures the importance of a feature based on its presence in different classes of documents and is given by Equation (19):

$$BNS\left(f_i\right) = \left| F^{-1}\left(\frac{C_P}{C_j}\right) - F^{-1}\left(\frac{C_N}{C_{j^{-1}}}\right) \right| \tag{19}$$

where,

F^{-1}: It is the inverse cumulative probability function of standard normal distribution.

$\dfrac{C_P}{C_j}$: True positive rate for a feature.

$\dfrac{C_N}{C_{j^{-1}}}$: False positive rate for the feature.

Since BNS scores are calculated over binary classes, we have used one vs rest all classes approach to signify positive and negative classes. It is important to note that the BNS score will tend to ∞ if either of the true positive rate or false rate becomes 1 or 0, Hence they are restricted between 0.0005 and 1-0.0005 as proposed (Forman, George, 2003; Forman, George, 2008).

B.11.3. Term Frequency-Inverse Document Frequency (TF-IDF)

It is a numerical statistic to find out how important a word is in a set of documents. It is obtained by multiplying the term frequency of the feature with the inverse of its document frequency and is given by Equation (20).

$$tfidf\left(f_i\right) = tf\left(f_i, d_j\right) * idf\left(f_i, D\right) \tag{20}$$

where,

$tf(f_i, d_j)$: Number of times a feature is present in the document d_j.

$idf(f_i, D)$: Inverse of the document frequency given by $\log\left(\dfrac{N}{D}\right)$

N: Total number of documents.

D: Number of documents in which feature f_i is present.

B.11.4. Term Frequency Bi-Normal separation (TF.BNS)

It was proposed in (Forman, George, 2008), and is calculated by multiplying the term frequency of the feature with its BNS score as per Equation (21):

$TF.BNS(f_i) = tf(f_i, d_j) * BNS(f_i)$ (21)

DF can be used for feature scoring and selected the top features based on document frequency score for each class after filtering out any features common to both classes. Mere presence of a feature in different classes is not enough for it to be discarded and may lead to loss of some good features. We can assign score to each feature and use an independent metric for feature selection. This may show good results in the classification results.

B.12. Feature Selection

Feature selection is carried out to convert the feature set to a manageable size and reduce the dimensionality of the features set to remove redundant and noisy feature which reduce the performance of the classification. Here, we carry out feature selection via filtering and have used two feature selection metrics which are commonly used. They are defined below:

B.12.1. Information Gain (IG)

It gives out the decrease in entropy for any feature caused due to it being present or absent in a document class and is widely used as feature selection metric (Furnkranz, Johannes, Tom Mitchell, and Ellen Riloff, 1998). It is given by Equation (22):

$$IG(f_m, C) = \sum_{i=0}^{j} -C_i \ln C_i - \sum_{q=\{0,1\}} \frac{|C_{q|}|}{|C|} \sum_{i=0}^{j} -C_i \ln C_i \qquad (22)$$

where,

f_m: m^{th} feature.
C: Number of documents.
j: Number of classes.
C_i: Number of documents belonging to class i.
C_q: Number of documents containing the feature f_m
C_i: Number of documents of class i containing f_m.
J: Presence or absence of a feature. It can be either 0 if absent or 1if present.

B.12.1. Chi-Square ($\chi2$) Test

The $\chi2$ test is used to test the independence of two variables. The $\chi2$ test measures the independence of a feature and a category. Features with the higher $\chi2$ values are less independent for a category, and bound to perform better for classification (Furnkranz, Johannes, Tom Mitchell, and Ellen Riloff, 1998). It is given by Equation (23):

$$\varsigma 2\left(f_i\right) = \sum_{i=1}^{n} \frac{\left(O_i - E_i\right)^2}{E_i} \tag{23}$$

where,

O_i: Observed value of feature i
E_i: Expected value of feature i

B.13. Performance of Classifier

The classifier's performance is measured in terms of the *error rate*. The prediction of classifier about the class of each sample is assessed. Correct prediction is counted as a *success*; and wrong prediction is counted as an *error*. Error rate - fraction of prediction errors made over a whole set of samples, measures the overall performance of the classifier. The classifications of each instance in the training set, is known hence; the error rate on old data cannot be used as an indicator of future performance The error rate on the training data is called the *resubstitution error* as it is calculated by resubstituting the training instances into a classifier that was constructed from them.

To predict the performance of a classifier on new data, we need to assess its error rate on a independent dataset called test dataset. Here, we assume that both the training data and the test data are representative samples of the underlying problem. It is important that the test data to be distinct in nature from the training data and is *not used in any way* to create the classifier. Three different datasets are chosen independently i.e. the *training* data for classifiers learning, the *validation* data-to optimize parameters of learnt classifier, and the *test* data for optimized learnt classifiers error calculation. For better classification and accurate error estimation, larger training and test sample is needed. Generally, one-third of the data is used for testing and the remaining two-thirds of the data used for training phase. To prevent any bias caused by the particular sample chosen, different random samples are chosen for each time and training/testing phase is repeated. Similarly, in case of cross-validation, the data is split into certain approximately equal partitions; each in turn is used for testing and the remainder is used for training.

Table 2. Two Class Prediction

Actual Class		Predicted Class	
		Ham	Spam
	Ham	True Positive	False Negative
	spam	False Positive	True Negative

In two-class predictions for e.g. ham or spam, any single prediction has the four different possible outcomes as shown in Table 2.

Here, the true positives (TP) are correct classifications of ham as a ham only. True negatives (TN) are correct classifications of spam as a spam only. A false positive (FP) is when a spam is incorrectly predicted as ham. A false negative (FN) is when a ham is incorrectly predicted as spam. The other parameters are:

1. True positive rate $(TPR) = \dfrac{TP}{TP + FN}$;

2. False positive rate $(FPR) = \dfrac{FP}{FP + TN}$;

3. The overall success rate is the number of correct classifications divided by the total number of classifications i.e.

   $(SuccessRate) = \dfrac{TP + TN}{TP + TN + FP + FN}$ and

4. Error Rate $= 1 -$ Success Rate.

In multiclass prediction, the result on a test set is often displayed as a two dimensional confusion matrix with a row and column for each class. Each matrix element shows the number of test examples for which the actual class is the row and the predicted class is the column. A graphical technique called as *receiver operating characteristic (ROC) that* characterizes the tradeoff between TPR (on Y axis) and FPR (on X axis) of a classifier without regard to class distribution or error costs.

REFERENCES

Das & Prasad. (2014). Analysis Of An Image Spam In Email Based On Content Analysis. *International Journal on Natural Language Computing, 3*(3).

Forman, G. (2003). An extensive empirical study of feature selection metrics for text classification. *Journal of Machine Learning Research, 3*, 1289–1305.

Forman, G. (2008). BNS feature scaling: an improved representation over tf-idf for svm text classification.*Proceedings of the 17th ACM conference on Information and knowledge management.* ACM. doi:10.1145/1458082.1458119

Furnkranz, J., Mitchell, T., & Riloff, E. (1998). A case study in using linguistic phrases for text categorization on the WWW. *Working Notes of the AAAI/ ICML, Workshop on Learning for Text Categorization.*

Salton, G., & Buckley, C. (1988). Term-weighting approaches in automatic text retrieval. *Information Processing & Management, 24*(5), 513–523. doi:10.1016/0306-4573(88)90021-0

Witten, I. H., Frank, E., & Hall, M. A. (2011). Data Mining - Practical Machine Learning Tools and Techniques (3rd ed.). Morgan Kaufmann Publishers.

About the Author

Sunita Vikrant Dhavale, presently associated with Defence Institute of Advanced Technology (DIAT), an autonomous institute under Ministry of Defence, Pune, as an Assistant Professor in Department of Computer Engineering. She received her M.E.(Computer Science Engineering) from the Pune University in 2009 and PhD (Computer Science Engineering) from DIAT University in 2015. She is recipient of IETE M. N. Saha Memorial Award for her paper published in IETE Journal of Research and Outstanding Woman Achiever Award from Venus International Foundation. She was selected as one of the top performers in four weeks AICTE approved Faculty Development Program on ICT tools by IIT, Bombay in September 2016. She has more than 20 publications in International Journals, International Conference proceedings and Book chapter. Her research areas are steganography, digital watermarking, multimedia forensics and security, cyber security. She organized first uniquely aimed National Conference on Electronics and Computer Engineering (NCECE - 2016) with the theme: Defence Applications in DIAT from 21st-22nd Jan 2016. She worked as a project manager for campus-wide Wi-Fi Project for higher research and education in DIAT in 2012. She emphasized on active learning strategy in her classroom. She arranged several seminars, workshops, Hands-on, presentation, debates, quizzes for providing the additional resources to MTech students and course improvement. She is member of many professional bodies including IEEE, ACM, ISTE, IETE, IAENG, and ISACA.

Index

  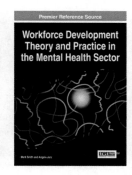 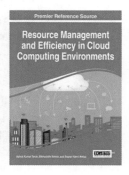

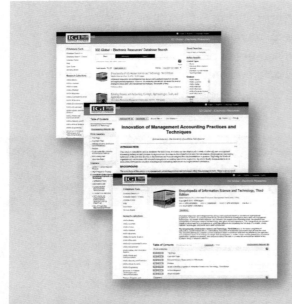

Printed in the United States
By Bookmasters